W9-ACG-690

THE APATHETIC MAJORITY

THE APATHETIC MAJORITY

A Study Based on Public Responses to the Eichmann Trial

BY

CHARLES Y. GLOCK, GERTRUDE J. SELZNICK,

AND

JOE L. SPAETH

HARPER & ROW, PUBLISHERS

New York, Evanston, and London

Volume Two in a series based on
The University of California Five-Year Study of Anti-Semitism
in the United States,
being conducted by the Survey Research Center
under a grant from the Anti-Defamation League of B'nai B'rith

FIRST EDITION

LIBRARY OF CONGRESS CATALOG CARD NUMBER: 64–7833

I-Q

CONTENTS

TABLES

Appendix Tables

PREFACE

THIS is the second volume of a series reporting the results of the University of California Five-Year Study of Anti-Semitism in the United States inaugurated in 1961 under a grant from the Anti-Defamation League of B'nai B'rith.

The original plans for the program provided for five basic, large-scale studies, each focusing on a different facet of the general phenomenon of anti-Semitism. The first of these, *Christian Beliefs and Anti-Semitism,* has already appeared. The other studies—on the vicissitudes of prejudice during adolescence, on political anti-Semitism, on anti-Semitism among Negroes, and on the extent and sources of anti-Semitism in the United States as a whole—will make up future volumes in the series. In addition to these studies, provision was also made to study ongoing events that had a special and immediate bearing on the problems of anti-Semitism. A special "firehouse" fund was set aside for this purpose, to be used for research on events as they were happening.

On receipt of the grant, the question immediately arose as to whether an event already in progress—the Eichmann trial —did not warrant an initial investment of firehouse funds. By the middle of 1961, the trial had occupied the world's headlines for over a year. Its manifest purpose was to remind the world of the Nazi atrocities and to create a body of public opinion armed against a repetition of such horrors. If anything might serve to inform world opinion about the evils of anti-Semitism, the Eichmann trial seemed to be an ideal medium for that purpose.

It was decided, therefore, to make the trial's impact on public opinion the subject of a special study. This book is the result.

The authors are grateful to the Anti-Defamation League of B'nai B'rith for making this study possible. Special thanks are due Mr. Benjamin Epstein, the League's director, and Mr. Oscar Cohen, its program director, for stimulating and initiating the larger program of which this work is a part.

Professor and Mrs. Leo Lowenthal and Mr. Earl Raab read the manuscript in several of its drafts, and their constructive criticisms have been immensely useful to us. Mr. Taylor Buckner and Mr. Stephen Steinberg served as research assistants to the project. Mr. Buckner took major responsibility for supervising the collection of data and organizing the coding and data-processing operations. Mr. Steinberg, besides contributing his editorial skills, was responsible for final tabulations and for preparing the material reported in Appendix B. We are indebted to them for more than their assistance on details. Each made thoughtful suggestions throughout the analysis, and we owe many insights to them. We wish also to thank Mr. William Nicholls II for technical advice in the design of the sample.

We are glad to have this opportunity to thank the Survey Research Center field unit, supervised at the time by Mrs. Ursula Fink, and its data-processing unit, then directed by Mr. Roderick Fredrickson. To Mrs. Lynne Alexander goes our special gratitude for typing the manuscript with dispatch and intelligence.

CHARLES Y. GLOCK
GERTRUDE J. SELZNICK
JOE L. SPAETH

Berkeley, California
April 1, 1966

THE APATHETIC MAJORITY

CHAPTER I

INTRODUCTION

THE startling capture of Adolf Eichmann, fifteen years after the fall of the Third Reich, attracted worldwide attention. The events of his capture and the circumstances of his trial were reported, analyzed, and debated before the American people for more than a year. Yet for all the coverage that the mass media allotted to the trial, one crucial question remained unanswered: What was the impact of the trial upon public opinion?

The declared purpose of the trial was to bring a criminal to justice, but the trial was also seen as a vehicle for informing public opinion. By recalling the barbaric mass murders engineered by Eichmann and his associates, it would recall to the world the demonic nature of Nazism in particular and political anti-Semitism in general, both of which had been countenanced by the German people and, to some extent, by the world at large. This reminder, it was hoped, would create a world climate of opinion that would preclude such events from happening again. The aim of the trial was to inform, but to inform the hearts as well as the minds of a possibly forgetful world.

Israel's concern that the trial serve a pedagogical purpose was mirrored in the coverage it received in the mass media. Despite occasional expressions of misgivings, the mass media reflected an almost universal identification with the larger goals of the trial. In fact, every major event of the trial produced a round of concerned speculation in the popular press as to what its effect would be on public opinion. Would sympathy for the trial's goals be endangered by the abduction of Eichmann from a Buenos Aires suburb? Would the public understand Israel's motive in wanting to try Eichmann herself? Would the court's sentence of death alienate those opposed to capital punishment? Editorials were often given over to airing possible doubts about the trial only to defend the legitimacy of Israel's actions.

In view of the avowed educational aims of the trial and worldwide concern that the trial succeed in its objectives, it seems reasonable to suppose that some effort would have been made to assess the trial's impact on public opinion. As far is is known, Israel herself made no effort to discover what and how much information was being communicated to the general public nor what the effect of such information was.[1] The mass media, though concerned, gathered no systematic information on the actual impact of the trial. Aside from a few questions asked in several Gallup polls—these will be noted later—no evidence was collected on the public's exposure and receptivity to the trial.

It may seem virtually inconceivable that the trial could have produced anything but a positive effect on public opinion. To be sure, it may have failed to elicit equal attention from all segments of the community. But among those whom it did reach, the possibility that some would not be persuaded by its message seems unlikely indeed. Who, knowing of the horrors perpetrated by the Nazis, could condone them? Who could ever wish them to be repeated?

Had these been the only issues raised by the trial, a good

[1] Dr. Akiva Deutsch, professor of sociology at Bar Ilan University in Ramat Gan, Israel, is currently conducting a study of the long-run impact of the trial among active Israeli army units. The results of this study were not available at the time that the present volume went to press.

deal of optimism would undoubtedly be justified concerning its impact. However, as the trial unfolded, the public was inexorably drawn into making judgments not only about the evils of Nazism but about the morality and wisdom of the trial itself. In the absence of well-established and prescribed legal channels, Israel had taken upon herself the responsibility of bringing Eichmann to justice. To a certain extent this placed Israel herself before the bar of public opinion. The trial was, moreover, not a single event, to be approved or disapproved in a blanket judgment. It was a long series of events extending from the scene of Eichmann's capture to the gallows at Jerusalem. At every point, Israel's actions were subject to evaluation.

However worthy and tenable Israel's goals, the means she adopted to achieve them were not always unambiguous. On some issues the ambiguity was grounded in questions having to do with international law. Was it legal that an Israeli court try Eichmann? And what about Israel's violation of Argentina's sovereignty? Sometimes the ambiguity arose around questions of tactics. Was it wise for Israel to focus attention on Eichmann's individual guilt? Would this not obscure the collective guilt of the German people, and, indeed, of a whole world that had done nothing to prevent the Nazi atrocities? Finally, in the discussions of Eichmann's punishment, moral considerations combined with legal and tactical ones to further confound the ambiguity. Did Israel, whose basic law forbids capital punishment, have the right to sentence Eichmann to death? Would death perhaps be too lenient a punishment? Would Eichmann's death be seen as expiating the crimes for which a whole generation, both inside and outside Germany, bore responsibility?

The ambiguities surrounding the Eichmann trial were probably inevitable. Once Israel had set out on the course of trying Eichmann herself, she could have done little to avoid them. That some of her actions were questionable was recognized by Israeli Premier Ben-Gurion when he invoked a "higher morality" to justify Eichmann's capture in Argentina.[2] In arranging that capture, in deciding to try Eichmann, and in publicizing the trial as she did, Israel took a calculated risk. She gambled that world opinion would not be alienated from the larger purposes of the trial by the ambiguities inherent in its conduct.

The extent of Israel's success remains unassessed, however.[3] The ambiguities of the trial may well have been overlooked by large segments of the public. For those who recognized them, one possible course was simply to resolve any perceived ambiguity in Israel's favor. But, where the ambiguities were not resolved in this way, where Israel's position on the issues of sovereignty, legality, guilt, and punishment were rejected or only partially accepted, what then? Perhaps the validity of the ends would transcend whatever concern the public might have about the means. On the other hand, concentration on the means might so obscure the ends as to result in their not being communicated, much less comprehended.

The foregoing seems to imply that the ends did not share the ambiguity of the means. This, too, cannot be taken for granted. It is true that statements of the trial's goals were made by Ben-Gurion and other Israeli officials. Newspaper editorials expatiated upon these statements, particularly with respect to the educational purposes of the trial. Nevertheless, the public was free to make its own interpretations of the goal of the trial and of Israel's motives in conducting it. Here again Israel gambled that, despite the ambiguous nature of some of her actions, her motives would nevertheless be under-

[2] David Ben-Gurion, *The New York Times Magazine,* December 18, 1960, VI.

[3] An examination of the impact of the trial based on two Gallup poll questions has since appeared in Irving Crespi, "Public Reaction to the Eichmann Trial," *Public Opinion Quarterly,* Spring 1964, XXVIII, No. 1, pp. 91–103.

stood, and in the way that she intended. Whether she gambled correctly is perhaps the ultimate question to be answered about the trial.

The decision to undertake this study was made in part out of a conviction that the impact of the trial on public opinion was an important question in its own right. It did not seem appropriate that the trial pass into history without some systematic effort to evaluate its effect. More than this, however, the authors were especially concerned to understand the requirements for counteracting the virus of anti-Semitism. The Eichmann trial was a monumental effort to combat anti-Semitism by reminding the world, in horrible and painful detail, of the consequences that lurk in anti-Semitism. There are lessons to be learned about the prospects for and the obstacles to eliminating anti-Semitism from an assessment of the trial's successes and failures.

A complementary objective of the study was to contribute to general knowledge about the formation and transformation of public opinion. Surprisingly few studies have been made of the influence of news events on public attitudes. Public opinion polls are regularly conducted to discover the public's response to events, but these generally report only the distribution of responses to the questions asked. Sometimes responses are broken down by social class or political orientation. But polls tell us very little about how people come to respond as they do, nor do they seek to account in a systematic way for differences in response.

Four months before the Eichmann trial ended it was known from a Gallup poll that 87 per cent of the United States population had heard about the trial. But what does this mean? How many of this number paid more than casual attention to the trial? Who were the people who did not know of an event so widely reported on for over a year? On the assumption, perhaps, of finding virtual unanimity, Gallup did not ask his respondents whether they thought Eichmann was guilty. However, even with unanimity on the question, it is still necessary to ask what people thought Eichmann was guilty of. Still more basic are questions concerning how the proceedings affected people's attitudes toward those who were the victims of the Nazi atrocities. Did the trial "boomerang" by evoking latent hostility or did it create new sympathies? These are the kinds of questions which this book seeks to answer for the Eichmann trial.

But similar questions arise with respect to every important national or international news event. The civil rights struggle of American Negroes has been headline news for several years. As this book went to press, news of the Vietnam war dominated the headlines. But, which person can say with any authority who is being affected by this news, how deeply, in what direction, and with what consequences for public policy and private conduct?

In sum, there is still much to be learned about public opinion formation and change. Who has opinions on what kinds of issues and who does not? How do people arrive at different conclusions about the same event? What is public opinion anyway, and how should it be regarded by public officials in the formulation of public policy? A study of the Eichmann trial cannot answer these questions for all kinds of events and for all kinds of circumstances. However, the answers obtained for the trial are relevant to a general understanding of the dynamics of public opinion formation as well as to understanding the significance of this event in the continuing struggle to combat anti-Semitism.

The Study: How and Where it Was Done

The study is based on 463 hour-long interviews with a representative sample of the population of Oakland, California, in the summer of 1961.[4] By then, the trial proceedings were nearly completed, the case for and against Eichmann was being summarized by the attorneys for the prosecution and the defense, and the court was about to adjourn to consider its verdict. The respondents were thus being asked about their reactions to the trial at a time when all the evidence was in, but before a verdict had been reached or a sentence imposed. In a sense, they were in a position akin to that of a jury. The interview became the vehicle through which they announced their verdict.

The decision to focus the study on the single city of Oakland offered the advantage that the study could be undertaken in greater depth and detail than would have been possible elsewhere. The investigators were familiar with the city's characteristics and with the mass media serving it. In fact, they had their own exposure to the trial primarily through the same media, and it was thought that this would be of help in interpreting the results.

No claim can be made that Oakland is a representative or typical American city. Nor can it be claimed that the sample chosen is representative of the American people as a whole. A nationwide study would have overcome this disadvantage. However, a sample of the national population would have been exposed to a great variety of local newspaper treatments of the trial, not to speak of the other mass media. It would have been difficult to sort out whether a particular difference in response was due to differences in the media content to which people were exposed or to some other factor.

In a few instances it was possible to compare the responses of the Oakland sample with those of a national sample interviewed by the Gallup poll. As will be seen, the two sets of answers are highly congruent. The authors are of the view that the processes of public opinion formation revealed by the

[4] The sample design is described in Appendix A.

present study are not limited to Oakland, but are applicable to the American population as a whole, and to literate populations generally. However, the test of whether or not the findings are relevant for other social environments can come only through replication of the kind of study reported here. For the present, the reader must bear in mind that the data were collected in Oakland and refer only to the population of that city.

In 1960 Oakland had a population of close to 370,000 people. Located across the bay from San Francisco, Oakland has been described as having a relation to that city akin to Newark's relation to New York City. Like Newark, Oakland is highly industrialized and has a large working-class population. Its middle class is composed largely of white-collar employees and merchants. Though it has a symphony orchestra and a few small museums, Oakland relies primarily on San Francisco for its cultural life.

Oakland has only one daily newspaper—the *Oakland Tribune*. San Francisco has two daily newspapers, and both—the *Chronicle* and the *Examiner*—have a considerable circulation in Oakland. The short-lived *New York Times Western Edition* was not in existence when the study was done. The city is served by well over twenty Bay Area radio stations, including the renowned Pacifica Foundation station KPFA, and five television channels, one of which, KQED, is an educational channel. Oaklanders have the same access to national magazines as anyone else. All in all, opportunities for exposure to the more sophisticated mass media, while inferior to those existing in New York City or Washington, D.C., are at least as good as and, because of local educational radio and television, perhaps slightly better than those existing in most metropolitan areas of the country.

At the time of the 1960 census, Oakland had a larger proportion of Negroes in its population than did the nation—

22.8 per cent as compared to a national average of 10.5 per cent. Only about 1 per cent of its present population is Jewish, as compared to a national average of 3 per cent. Roman Catholics account for 22 per cent, Protestants for 67 per cent of the population.[5] The foreign-born are proportionately fewer than in many urban areas in other parts of the country; in this respect Oakland resembles other cities in the West. During World War II, many Southerners—both Negro and white—migrated to Oakland in search of employment in its industries, and many have remained. The dominant strains in the ethnic background of Oakland's population are Anglo-Saxon, Italian, German, and Mexican.[6] In income and education, Oakland compares favorably with other urban centers in the United States. According to the 1960 census, half of the families in Oakland earned an annual income of above $6,303. The comparable figure for urban centers in the coterminous United States was $6,166. The median number of school years completed was 11.4 for Oaklanders, as compared to 11.0 for the urban United States.

The questions asked in the interview appear in Appendix C. As the reader can see, they were designed to discover the amount and kind of attention given to the trial, to obtain reactions to specific events of the trial, and to learn how much and what part of Israel's message was absorbed and accepted. Because of the study's special interest in assessing the bearing of anti-Semitism on reactions to the trial, the questionnaire

[5] Estimates of the religious distribution of the Oakland population are based on the present study. Protestants and Catholics are found in about the same proportions as in the country as a whole. At the time of the 1957 census report on religious bodies, 66 per cent of the American population were Protestant, 26 per cent were Catholic, and 3 per cent were Jewish (U.S. Bureau of the Census, *Current Population Reports,* Series P-20, No. 79, February 2, 1958).

[6] According to the 1960 census, 28.2 per cent of Oakland's population are of foreign stock (immigrants or children of immigrants). Among these, 10.6 per cent migrated from England, 10.3 per cent from Italy, 9.6 per cent from Germany, and 7.7 per cent from Mexico.

included a variety of measures of anti-Semitism and other forms of prejudice.

As is true of most studies based on interviews with a sample population, the analysis revealed to the investigators that they did not have the foresight to ask all of the right questions. On certain matters that proved on hindsight to be important the analysis suffers from the absence of the appropriate data. By and large, however, the questionnaire proved to be an adequate instrument for its purpose.

The book is structured to follow the process through which public opinion about the trial developed. It begins by analyzing exposure, proceeds to an examination of attitudes toward different aspects of the trial, and ends with a consideration of the trial's lasting effects.

Chapter 2 answers four questions about exposure: How much attention did the trial receive from the citizens of Oakland? Was this attention of a kind to suggest that the trial was viewed as an event of special significance? Who was reached, and who was not? And, specifically, to what extent did it engage those with a proclivity toward anti-Semitism? More generally, the chapter asks to what extent public opinion is grounded in knowledge and interests.

Chapters 3, 4, and 5 consider, in turn, public response to three main trial issues: Was Eichmann guilty and, if so, of what? Was the trial legal? And, what should Eichmann's punishment be? The public approached such issues, as all issues, from different social contexts, with different degrees of sophistication, and armed with varying amounts of information. The chapters seek to answer for the trial itself, and for public issues more generally, how such factors influence the way opinion is formed.

Chapter 6 evaluates the success of the trial in achieving its educational aims. Did it actually inform the population of the extent of the Nazi atrocities of the 1930s and 1940s? Did it succeed in creating a climate of opinion favorable to Jews and to Israel? This chapter also considers how attitudes interacted with knowledge and social position to determine the public's ultimate judgments of the trial.

In a concluding chapter some observations are made about the lessons to be learned from the trial both for the continuing battle against anti-Semitism and for a broader understanding of public opinion processes.

The Course of the Trial: A Reminder

It is assumed throughout the book that the reader is familiar with the details of the trial and the events leading up to it. Nevertheless, as a reminder, it might be helpful to outline briefly the sequence of events.

The Eichmann case first came to the world's attention on the morning of May 24, 1960. On that day Israeli Premier David Ben-Gurion announced that Adolf Eichmann had been found, was being held in Israel, and would be tried for his crimes by an Israeli court. The initial announcement did not provide details about the manner or the location of the capture. However, within a week the Israeli government confirmed that Eichmann had been taken by its agents from a suburb of Buenos Aires, Argentina, and brought to Israel on Foreign Minister Abba Eban's El Al airliner. Few news analysts took seriously Israel's *pro forma* statement that Eichmann had not been kidnaped, but had submitted willingly; most accepted the unofficial explanation that Israel had kidnaped Eichmann because of Argentina's past refusals to extradite ex-Naxis discovered within its territory.

The so-called kidnaping, which was in violation of an extradition treaty signed only two days earlier, was officially protested by Argentina. The issue was subsequently taken to the United Nations Security Council where Israel was chided for the capture, but not directed to return Eichmann to Argentina.

After the Security Council resolution in June 1960, Israel began to make preparations for the trial. The charges against Eichmann were drawn up. Arrangements for press and television coverage of the trial were made. Through a series of public statements, Israel outlined its purposes in conducting the trial.

In February 1961 fifteen charges against Eichmann were revealed. The first eight pertained to Eichmann's crimes against Jews and against humanity. The next four accused Eichmann of crimes against non-Jewish groups, specifically, Poles, Slavs, and gypsies. The last three charges accused him of membership in organizations branded as illegal by the Nuremberg trial.

At the end of February, the composition of the court was announced. The three members were Benjamin Halevi, a judge in the Jerusalem District Court; Itzhak Raveh, a judge in the Tel Aviv District Court; and Moshe Landau, a justice of Israel's Supreme Court, who was named chairman. Earlier, the Knesset, Israel's parliament, had voted to pay German lawyer Robert Servatius to defend Eichmann. Attorney General Gideon Hausner accepted responsibility for the prosecution.

The trial opened on April 10, 1961, with the indictment against Eichmann. Servatius immediately challenged Israel's illegal abduction of Eichmann and her right to try, and charged that the court was prejudiced against Eichmann. Hausner replied that no court in the world could fail to be biased against Eichmann, but that prejudice would not be permitted to enter into the proceedings. The court denied Servatius's objections and held that Israel did have jurisdiction. Eichmann pleaded not guilty to all fifteen counts of the indictment, partly on the ground that he had been a mere subordinate carrying out official orders.

Hausner devoted part of his opening statement to a summary of the evidence showing that Eichmann did more than follow orders. He described Eichmann's role in the deportation of German and Austrian Jews in 1938, and his statement summarized the Nazi mass executions and tortures, including the death march of Hungarian Jews organized by Eichmann in 1944.

From the middle of April to the middle of June, Hausner introduced evidence of Nazi crimes and Eichmann's complicity in them. Survivors of the pogroms, the shootings, the labor camps, and the death camps told of their experiences. They told not only of the organized slayings but of gratuitous and sadistic torture. Some of the evidence did not mention Eichmann by name, but the court held such information to be relevant because it sought to show not only that crimes had been committed but that they had been of a particularly heinous nature. Much of the testimony dealt with Eichmann directly.

In late June and July, Eichmann himself testified. Servatius's examination tried to establish that Eichmann had been no more than a bureaucrat following orders and that he had actually shown kindness to Jews when he could. Hausner's cross-examination persistently sought to destroy this image. Eichmann was continually confronted with documents describing his activities; some of these documents contained his own signature. At the beginning of the cross-examination Eichmann admitted his "moral guilt" in the slaying of European Jewry, but this merely served as an argument that he was an accessory, not a perpetrator. Before his testimony ended, he admitted that the slaughter of Jews was a "hideous crime," but he continued to maintain that he was merely following orders and that it was his duty to do so.

Eichmann's testimony ended with an examination by the judges on July 25, 1961. The early weeks in August were occupied with the summations of prosecution and defense. The court then recessed until December. On December 10, Eichmann was convicted on all fifteen counts. On December 14, he was sentenced to hang, but was granted the right to appeal to the Israeli Supreme Court. His appeal was unanimously rejected by this five-man tribunal on May 28, 1962. Eichmann's appeal to President Itzhak Ben-Zvi was also rejected. He was hanged on May 30, 1962, and his ashes, in an act that symbolized the dissolution of Nazi racism, were scattered over the Mediterranean.

CHAPTER 2

EXPOSURE TO THE TRIAL

PUBLIC opinion is a familiar and widely used concept whose meaning may seem to be simple and transparent. In all probability, few readers paused in Chapter 1 to ask what the authors had in mind when they used the term. Public opinion is one of a class of commonly used concepts which have been specified sufficiently so that something is communicated when they are used in everyday conversation; the flow of conversation does not stop because people feel obliged to consider definitions. If one insists on a precise rendering of the idea, however, public opinion turns out to be a very fuzzy concept indeed.

Since the advent of polling, public opinion has commonly been conceived as that which is reported in the results of polls. This conception of public opinion—as the summation of what a population thinks about an issue or a set of issues—seems straightforward and unambiguous. It also seems especially appropriate for the present study since this, too, is based on a poll.

The matter is not so simple, however. Problems and complexities begin to mount from the moment that analysis of polling data begins. The first question that arises concerns what to do with those people who, when queried, reply that they do not have an opinion on the issue at hand. This might appear to present no problem, requiring simply that the concept of public opinion be modified to exclude the "don't knows." Thus public opinion would denote only the opinions of those in the population who are able and willing to express an opinion. For some purposes this might be a reasonable and unobjectionable definition. On many occasions, however, it means omitting a considerable portion of the public from one's conception of public opinion.

But the problems do not stop with the "don't knows." Looking at those who have expressed themselves in one way or another, the question arises as to whether everyone who says he has an opinion really has one. People often do not think about an issue until they are asked their opinion about it. Under these circumstances, some respondents will refuse to express themselves. But many people are unable to live with a conception of themselves as opinionless. Stimulated by a question, they form an opinion on the spot.

Further confounding matters is the fact that opinions need not be informed. Some people are ready to express an opinion on the basis of relatively little or no knowledge while others will not do so until they have given careful thought and consideration to the facts. Common sense also tells us that opinions may be stable or unstable and that some people change their minds out of conviction while others bend readily with the prevailing winds of doctrine.

Again the implications must be considered. Should thoughtful, informed, and stable opinions be distinguished in some way from uninformed, on-the-spot, and unstable opinions? In some cases it may not seem necessary to do so, for example, when a poll is inquiring into the nation's presidential preferences. According to the democratic principle of one man, one vote, every ballot counts equally no matter what its source and no matter what the quality of the voting decision. But even in pre-election polls it is a wise procedure to sort out informed from uninformed opinions, stable from unstable choices. Not all people actually vote; and it is important to know whether the uninformed will show the same tendency to stay at home on election day that they have often shown in the past. It is also important to try to discover how many people will change their minds before election day. Otherwise, prediction of the outcome of the election may be inaccurate. But voting studies merely illustrate the problem. To know whether the population has formed genuine opinions, and whether these are informed or uninformed, stable or unstable judgments, seems essential to all assessments of public opinion.

Already the concept of public opinion has become complex. However, one further subtlety must be mentioned. It is well to remember that, in many matters, not everyone's opinion counts equally. Some segments of the population are in a better position to influence policy than others. Some people are more active than others in promulgating their beliefs and in getting them listened to. Thus it is often vital to know not only what opinions are held and how many people hold them, but who believes what. Minority opinion, if it is held by an influential or vocal group, may be more weighty in determining policy and the future course of public sentiment than majority opinion.

These issues, relevant to any general discussion of public opinion, are especially germane to a study of the impact of the Eichmann trial on public opinion. To take one example, a judicious estimate of the success of the trial depends upon knowing whether informed opinion reacted to the trial differently from uninformed opinion. For instance, people were not all persuaded in a uniform way of the propriety of Israel's actions. But where did disapproval come from? From those who evidenced familiarity with the full story of the trial or from those with little or no knowledge of the facts? And who were the disapprovers? Were they people of some stature and influence in the community, whose opinion might count for a great deal? In studying the impact of the Eichmann trial it would be superficial to count opinions as if they were votes for or against the trial. It is necessary to probe more deeply, to ask who had what kinds of opinions and whether these opinions were informed or uninformed. Beyond that some attempt must also be made to assess the depth of conviction with which the various opinions and attitudes were held.

Before opinion about the issues of the trial can be examined, a number of preliminary questions must be considered. These questions concern the amount of public attention that the trial received and the intensity with which it was attended to. It cannot be taken for granted that everyone was even aware that the trial was going on, much less that everyone was equally interested in and informed about it. Extent of public awareness and knowledge of an event—in this case the Eichmann trial—becomes, then, the first criterion for assessing its impact. Without the public's being aware of the trial and interested enough to learn something about it, the educational purposes of the trial would be frustrated from the start. A second criterion, closely related to the first, is whether an event is singled out for special or extraordinary attention. The extent to which the Eichmann trial succeeded in its historic mission must be judged, at least in part, by the extent to which the trial loomed large in public consciousness as an event of special significance.

Awareness of the Trial

The citizens surveyed in this study did not lack for opportunities to become exposed to and informed about the Eichmann trial. The trial and the events leading up to it received prominent attention in area newspapers and on local radio stations. It was the subject of several national television programs heard in the area. It was featured in stories in mass circulation magazines—*Life, Time, Look, Reader's Digest*—and in more sophisticated journals of opinion—*Harper's, Atlantic Monthly, Reporter, Saturday Review*. In addition, there was the possibility of hearing about it through conversations with neighbors, friends, coworkers.

Not all of these sources of information were available to everyone, but all the persons interviewed were in touch with at least one source of information. Eighty-six per cent reported that they regularly read one of the major newspapers of the area. Fifty-seven per cent were regular readers of magazines that carried some kind of report on the trial and Israel's capture of Eichmann. Respondents were not asked whether they owned a radio or television set, but the Bureau of the Census reports that, in 1960, 89 per cent of the residents of Alameda County, California, which includes Oakland, the home of those in the study, owned at least one television set and 91 per cent owned at least one radio.

Opportunity for exposure to an event does not automatically lead to actual exposure. In the sample there were 74 people, or 16 per cent of the total, who reported that they had never heard of the trial. The vast majority—84 per cent—did meet the minimum criterion of simple awareness. This figure is almost identical with the 87 per cent who, in a Gallup poll conducted in April 1961, indicated they were aware that the trial was going on.

Many may wonder how it was possible for one out of six Oaklanders to have managed to escape exposure to an event that had been in the news for over a year. Others, familiar with past data on levels of public knowledge, may find it surprising that as many as 84 per cent had heard about the trial. In order to set the figure of 84 per cent in proper perspective, it is necessary to compare the amount of attention given to the Eichmann trial with that given to other news events of the day.

In the early summer of 1961, when the interviews were

being collected, the headlines were occupied with the usual mixture of reports about local, national, and international events, news about the nation's celebrities, and human interest stories. The Freedom Riders were active in the South. Lincoln Rockwell, head of the American Nazi Party, was attempting to counteract the Freedom Riders by driving through the South in what came to be called a "hate bus." The initial tractors-for-rebels exchange with Cuba was at the height of what later turned out to be an abortive negotiation. Ernest Hemingway and Gary Cooper had recently died. Marilyn Monroe was having an operation.

Compared to these other events of the day, the Eichmann trial did not get an unusual amount of attention. More people knew about the Freedom Riders (93 per cent) and the death of Gary Cooper (93 per cent) than knew about the trial (84 per cent). About the same proportion had heard of the tractors-for-rebels exchange with Cuba (86 per cent), Marilyn Monroe's operation (82 per cent), and Ernest Hemingway's death (82 per cent). The only item that attracted substantially less attention was Rockwell's hate bus (46 per cent) but, in contrast to the other stories, the Rockwell episode was never headline news.

According to this evidence, the trial was apparently not singled out for special attention by the public. On the simple criterion of awareness, it generated no more interest and attention than other major news events of the day. In fact, it accumulated less attention among respondents over the course of a year than Gary Cooper's death attracted in a few days. However, it would be a mistake to conclude from this that the trial had no special impact on those who did know about it.

The data on awareness provide an initial clue to the kind of news reader who knew of the trial and the kind who did not. The news events to which the Eichmann trial has just been compared were not all cut from the same cloth. Several —the tractors-for-rebels exchange, the Freedom Riders, the death of Ernest Hemingway—were events of more historical interest than the stories about Gary Cooper and Marilyn Monroe. Among those who were aware of the Eichmann trial the vast majority knew about the tractors-for-rebels exchange and also about Marilyn Monroe's operation. But, as shown in Table 1, they tended to be more aware of the serious news

TABLE 1. AWARENESS OF OTHER NEWS EVENTS BY AWARENESS OF EICHMANN TRIAL[a]

Per Cent Aware of:	Aware of Eichmann Trial	Not Aware of Trial	Percentage Point Difference
Death of Ernest Hemingway	90%	39%	51
Tractors-for-rebels exchange with Cuba	93	49	44
American Nazi "hate bus"	50	24	26
Death of Gary Cooper	96	73	23
Marilyn Monroe's operation	85	72	13
Number of respondents	(389)	(74)	

[a] The Freedom Riders event is omitted from this table. It constituted an exception for reasons to be explained in the text.

story (93 per cent) than of the less serious news story (85 per cent).[1] In contrast, those who were not aware of the trial were considerably more likely to know about Marilyn Monroe (72 per cent) than to know about the exchange (49 per cent). This relation is part of a general pattern. Those who attended to the trial were more interested in serious news events. Those who did not attend to the trial were more interested in less serious news events.

[1] With the presentation of the first table, it is appropriate to remark that the significance of statistical results has been evaluated with respect to both face validity and internal consistency. Formal tests of statistical significance have not been used on the grounds reported in Seymour M. Lipset, Martin A. Trow, and James S. Coleman, *Union Democracy: The Inside Politics of the International Typographical Union* (Glencoe, Ill.: The Free Press, 1956), pp. 427–432.

The trial, then, tended to be viewed as one among a class of more serious news events. There is no evidence that it was perceived as in any way distinctive within its class. Had the Eichmann trial been seen as especially noteworthy, it would have captured a disproportionate amount of attention from those not ordinarily interested in serious news events. But this was not the case. When respondents are classified into serious and nonserious news readers, there is nothing to suggest that the less serious overcame their usual reading habits to pay particular attention to the Eichmann trial.[2]

A high proportion of nonserious readers, however, was aware of the Freedom Riders. It may be instructive to consider this event for a moment to illustrate what is typically required to stimulate interest in and awareness of a news story among the nonserious reading public.

As was mentioned earlier, 93 per cent of the general public had heard of the Freedom Riders. However, a striking difference appears between the responses of the white and the Negro communities. Among white respondents 95 per cent of those who were aware of the trial were also aware of the Freedom Riders. Among those white respondents who had not heard of the trial this figure fell to 42 per cent. The situation in the Negro community was very different. Virtually every Negro respondent knew about the Freedom Riders whether or not he had heard of the Eichmann trial. Of those aware of the trial, 100 per cent knew about the Freedom Riders. But almost as many—96 per cent—had heard of the

[2] Considering as serious news readers those who were aware of at least three of the four serious news events (Eichmann, Hemingway, tractors, Freedom Riders) and nonserious readers those who were aware of fewer than three of these events, neither the serious nor the nonserious news readers showed any disproportionatae tendency to have been aware of the Eichmann trial. Among the serious news readers, 96 per cent knew of the trial; 93 per cent, of Hemingway; 98 per cent, of the tractors; and 99 per cent, of the Freedom Riders. Among the nonserious news readers, 25 per cent knew of the trial; 25 per cent, of Hemingway; 26 per cent, of the tractors; and 66 per cent, of the Freedom Riders.

Freedom Riders even when they had not heard of the trial. In the Negro community, the story of the Freedom Riders was so salient that it attracted the attention of both those who ordinarily give attention to serious news events and those who do not.

The reason for this is clear. A story of such great importance to Negroes transcended the usual conditions which determine the attention given to an event. The Eichmann trial was undoubtedly singled out for such special attention in the Jewish community; of the five Jews in the Oakland sample, all were aware of the trial.[3] Aside from this small group there is no evidence that awareness of the Eichmann trial was concentrated in any subgroup of the population that would ordinarily not have been aware of serious news events in general.

It can be concluded that the trial was seen as a serious news event and distinguished from events of a less serious nature. Thus it was attended to by the serious news reader and not noticed by the nonserious reader. It does not appear to have been conceived as unique within the general class of serious news events and as deserving of special attention.

Knowledge of the Trial and the Circumstances Leading Up to It

Awareness is only a minimal indicator of exposure to an event. It says nothing about the extent of people's knowledge and understanding. Regarding the Eichmann trial, some persons might have been aware of its existence only in the sense of vaguely remembering having heard or read about it somewhere. Others might have gained a profound knowledge and understanding of the trial in all its details. In order to assess the significance of awareness and to probe more deeply into

[3] The five Jewish cases, because of their special interest in the trial, are omitted from all further analysis.

the question of impact, it is essential to discover just how informed the "awares" actually were about the trial and the events leading up to it.

Four questions measuring knowledge of the trial were incorporated into the interview. In order not to confuse knowledge with opinion, care was exercised to ensure that the questions referred only to factual information. Two of these questions pertained to the capture: "Do you happen to remember in what country Eichmann was arrested?" "And what country arrested him?" One question dealt with Eichmann's identity: "Do you know whether Eichmann was a Communist, a Nazi, or a Jew?" A final question tapped knowledge of the Nazi persecutions: "An *official* estimate has been made of the number of Jews killed by the Nazis before and during World War II. Would you please look at this card and tell me which number comes closest to this official estimate?"

These questions could be asked only of those who said they had heard of the trial; in the following discussion, percentage figures refer to this group alone. The relevant tables, however, also report percentage figures based on the total sample. Since there are advantages and disadvantages to both procedures, results are presented in both forms.

Judging from the responses, one must conclude that the four factual questions gave the respondents considerable difficulty. Of the awares, one-third (32 per cent) replied correctly that Eichmann had been captured in Argentina (Table 2). Forty-one per cent said they did not know where Eichmann had been arrested. Another 27 per cent gave an incorrect answer. Since more than a year had elapsed between the event and the question about it, some, though certainly not all, of the incorrect or don't-know answers are undoubtedly attributable to failure of memory rather than to an original unawareness of the event.

That Israel had captured Eichmann was also stale news at

the time of the interviews. However, Israel was conducting the trial, and this special reminder and clue that she had

TABLE 2. KNOWLEDGE OF PLACE OF EICHMANN'S ARREST

	Those Aware of Trial	Total Sample
Correct answer: Argentina	32%	27%
Incorrect answers:		
South America	15	12
Other	12	10
Total incorrect answers	27	22
Don't know[a]	41	35
Had not heard of trial		16
Number of respondents	(384)	(458)

[a] In this and all subsequent tables, refusals to answer and no answers are included in the "don't know" category. In all cases, they constituted less than 1 per cent of the sample.

originally captured Eichmann probably accounts for the 50 per cent who knew this fact as compared with the 32 per cent who knew where the capture had occurred. Nevertheless, half the awares were either incorrectly informed or ignorant on this question (Table 3).

TABLE 3. KNOWLEDGE THAT STATE OF ISRAEL HAD ARRESTED EICHMANN

	Those Aware of Trial	Total Sample
Correct answer: Israel	50%	42%
Incorrect answers	11	9
Don't know	39	33
Had not heard of trial		16
Number	(384)	(458)

The most elementary of the four questions was the one asking for Eichmann's identity. That Eichmann was a Nazi was referred to over and over again as the trial ran its course. Knowledge of this fact was an essential prerequisite for minimal comprehension of the trial, its significance, and its lessons. Yet even though the question included the right answer among its choices, only 59 per cent of the awares replied correctly (Table 4). Twenty-one per cent said they did not

TABLE 4. KNOWLEDGE THAT EICHMANN WAS A NAZI

	Those Aware of Trial	Total Sample
Correct answer: Nazi	59%	50%
Incorrect answers:		
Communist	5	5
Jew	9	7
Other[a]	6	5
Total incorrect answers	20	17
Don't know	21	17
Had not heard of trial		16
Number	(384)	(458)

[a] Two per cent of these people said "German." The remainder gave pairs of two of the three identities named in the question, for example, Nazi-Communist.

know what Eichmann was. An additional 20 per cent gave an incorrect answer; contributing to this 20 per cent were 9 per cent who thought that Eichmann was a Jew.

The answer to the final question, which asked for the official estimate of the number of Jews killed by the Nazis, was also prominently featured in news reports of the trial proceedings. Just as the information that Eichmann was a Nazi was the most elementary fact that the trial had to communicate, the most elementary fact about the Nazi atrocities was that 6 million Jews had been killed.[4]

Despite the almost daily reiteration by the mass media of

[4] Though not all observers have accepted 6 million as the correct number, the mass media almost uniformly did. Hilberg estimates that 5.1 million Jews were slaughtered [see Raul Hilberg, *The Destruction of the European Jews* (Chicago: Quadrangle Press, 1961), p. 767]. Interestingly enough, according to Hilberg, the estimate of 6 million comes from Eichmann himself, made in a report to Himmler. The Nuremberg tribunal established 6 million as the official estimate.

the figure, only 33 per cent of the awares knew that the official estimate was 6 million (Table 5). Of the remainder, 56 per cent gave incorrect answers and 11 per cent did not venture a guess. Exact knowledge of the official estimate was

TABLE 5. KNOWLEDGE OF OFFICIAL ESTIMATE OF NUMBER OF JEWS KILLED BY THE NAZIS

	Those Aware of Trial	Total Sample
Correct answer: 6,000,000	33%	28%
Incorrect answers:		
10,000 or less	7	6
100,000	5	4
500,000	5	4
1,000,000	8	7
2,000,000	8	7
4,000,000	12	10
8,000,000	5	4
10,000,000	6	5
Total incorrect answers	56	47
Don't know	11	9
Had not heard of trial		16
Number	(384)	(458)

certainly not high among respondents. The figure of 33 per cent cannot be made to appear in any other light, especially when it is remembered that the correct response was included in the choices on the card handed to the respondent.

The impression conveyed by looking at the responses, question by question, is that the trial did not penetrate very broadly or deeply into the minds of the sample population. This impression is reinforced when the answers are considered in combination. Only 13 per cent of the awares answered all four knowledge questions correctly; 20 per cent had three correct answers, 20 per cent two, 23 per cent one, and 24 per cent none (Table 6).

These figures do not take into account those who had not even heard of the trial. When this group is included, a picture emerges that may seem, to many, distressing indeed. Combining the 16 per cent who had not heard of the trial with the

TABLE 6. NUMBER OF KNOWLEDGE QUESTIONS ANSWERED CORRECTLY[5]

Number Correct	Those Aware of Trial	Total Sample
Four	13%	11%
Three	20	17
Two	20	17
One	23	19
None	24	20
Had not heard of trial		16
Number	(384)	(458)

20 per cent who failed to answer any of the four questions correctly produces a total of 36 per cent who were not reached by the trial at all (Table 6, second column). This is more than three times as many people as knew the answers to all four questions.

To readers familiar with the results of other studies of public opinion, these figures may come as no surprise. It has been documented over and over again that the details of even the most publicized national and international events elude the majority of the public.[6] Only when an event has deep per-

[5] Intercorrelations (Q) between the responses to the four knowledge items are given here; the questions are labeled by their correct answers.

	Nazi	*Israel*	*Argentina*	*6 million*
Nazi		.71	.58	.40
Israel			.81	.56
Argentina				.71

[6] In April 1961, for example, only 37 per cent of Americans had heard of the by then widely publicized John Birch Society. During the protracted discussion of the Taft-Hartley legislation in the early 1950s, 53 per cent of the American population was the highest proportion who reported having heard of the law (see section on "The Polls" in the Winter 1962, Spring 1963, Fall 1963, and Winter 1963 issues of the *Public Opinion Quarterly* for reports on the extent of the American public's knowledge as measured by national polls since 1946).

sonal meaning for a population is lack of interest and concern overcome. The Freedom Riders was such an event for the Negro community of Oakland. The Eichmann trial undoubtedly had this quality for the Jewish population. But if extent of factual information is any test, then it must be said that the majority of the non-Jewish population of Oakland did not perceive the trial as personally relevant or interesting.

While this is the general conclusion to be drawn from the analysis so far, there are exceptions to the rule. For some people, though relatively few in number, the trial was of sufficient seriousness or interest to lead them to acquire the knowledge to answer all four questions correctly. What is true on the average—that the trial did not penetrate deeply into public consciousness—was not uniformly true. The majority of the sample knew little or nothing concerning the trial, but some people did evidence familiarity with the details on which they were questioned.

It is now possible to deepen and extend the analysis by investigating what kinds of people became knowledgeable. Were they different in any way from those who remained ignorant? In particular, did those with anti-Semitic tendencies follow the trial or did they avoid it?

Bases of Knowledgeability

The Eichmann trial was perceived by the public as one of a class of serious news events, but there is no evidence that it was singled out for extraordinary or unusual attention. In all probability most of the people who gave the trial enough attention to become relatively well informed about it were the same people who become informed about any serious news event.

Past research on public opinion has provided a portrait of the person who routinely attends to the news, whether it has deep personal significance for him or not. Piecing together the results of a wide variety of studies reveals a surprisingly consistent picture of the well-informed person. He is typically one of the more privileged members of society.[7]

However unconsciously it may do so, society makes invidious distinctions among individuals. On the basis of these distinctions, society distributes the privileges and rewards it has to offer in unequal ways. From some segments of the population it invites full participation in the affairs of society and rewards their involvement with status, economic privilege, and influence. With respect to other segments of the population, it not only fails to encourage full participation, but often actively discourages it. This is most clearly seen in the invidious racial distinctions which American society makes and in the many opportunities available to whites but closed to Negroes.

Other distinctions similarly serve to enlarge or restrict opportunities and rewards. Women, for example, are denied opportunities to engage in a wide variety of activities open to men. A whole set of distinctions centers around socio-economic status. People of superior education, people of means, people in managerial and professional occupations are invited to take important roles in managing the economic, political, and social life of society that are seldom open to those in less privileged positions. Even age plays its part in determining degree of involvement in the affairs of society. Pre-adults stand at the threshold of full social participation and are rarely given responsible roles to play. At the other extreme, the elderly often find themselves in the process of

[7] For example, in *The People's Choice,* Paul Lazarsfeld summarizes his findings with the following statement: "In short, the person most interested in the election is more likely to be found in urban areas among men on higher levels of education, with better socio-economic status, . . ." Lazarsfeld later shows that these factors are also associated with high exposure to political communications (New York: Columbia University Press, 1949, p. 45).

being excluded from full participation or of voluntarily withdrawing from social responsibility.

Many links exist between privileged participation in the workings of society and becoming well informed about the news. Not the least of these is the fact that those who are given the broadest opportunities to participate are the same people who are expected to be the best informed. A man is normally expected to be familiar with current events to a degree not expected of a woman, even when both have the same amount of education. A woman who evinces great familiarity with serious news events is apt to be looked upon with suspicion as possibly lacking in femininity. She may encounter negative rather than positive sanctions when she exhibits a high degree of knowledge. At the same time, the woman with a college education would normally be expected to know more about current events than the woman with only a high school education. In much the same way, the executive with a high school education would be expected to read the newspapers more seriously and intensively than the high school graduate who is a blue-collar worker. In general, with every increment in privilege, expectations rise as to the knowledgeability, seriousness, and sophistication which individuals should exhibit.

Those who are encouraged to participate fully in society are the same people who are urged to get a superior education and to become highly literate. Education is, by itself, one of the avenues to a privileged position. But it is also one of the advantages which the already privileged are likely to possess. More is expected of the privileged, but they are given the intellectual tools with which to fulfill the demands made upon them.

Still more important, perhaps, is the fact that the efforts of the privileged to gain knowledge, including knowledge about public affairs, do not go unrewarded. Those who are singled out for full participation in the larger society are given higher incomes and greater prestige than those not so favored. But in no small measure the extent to which the already privileged can rise still further depends on the extent to which they can demonstrate knowledgeability and sophistication concerning what is going on in the world. The opinions of the privileged count for something, if only to raise their status among their peers. In every respect, being well informed is functional for the privileged person.

For the less privileged person, on the other hand, being well informed has no particular value. It may do him no positive harm, but it is not apt to do him much good either. The essence of being disprivileged is that one occupies positions and roles to which high degrees of knowledge and sophistication of the kind being considered here are largely irrelevant.

Thus the very characteristics that encourage participation in the larger society are also those that encourage interest in public affairs. The truth of this observation has been confirmed repeatedly in studies of public opinion. Consistently it has been found that the educated more than the uneducated, the rich more than the poor, whites more than Negroes, men more than women, exhibit greater interest in and concern for public affairs, not in an idiosyncratic way but on all kinds of public issues. It takes a news event of immediate personal interest to overcome these tendencies. Most events do not have this quality; apparently the Eichmann trial was among them. One would expect, therefore, that social privilege is a major determinant of knowledge about the trial.

This expectation is immediately borne out when knowledgeability about the trial is examined by race. Whites were considerably more likely to be knowledgeable than Negroes. They were also more likely to be informed than the twenty persons classified as "other," mostly Orientals and Mexicans. The superior knowledgeability of the white respondents is evident no matter how the figures in Table 7 are grouped. Generally speaking, "others," while less likely to be knowledgeable than whites, were more likely to be so than Negroes. This, too, confirms expectations. In Oakland, Orientals and

TABLE 7. KNOWLEDGE OF TRIAL BY RACE[a]

Number of Correct Answers to Knowledge Questions	White	Negro	Other
Four	16%	3%	5%
Three	21	4	30
Two	21	8	15
One	19	21	15
None	17	30	0
Had not heard of trial	6	34	35
Number	(295)	(141)	(20)

[a] Two persons are omitted from this table because of lack of information concerning their race. Future discrepancies in number of respondents will generally not be noted since they are too small to affect the results.

Mexicans, who make up most of the so-called others, are more privileged than the Negro but have less status than the whites.

Much the same result is obtained when other factors are used to distinguish the more privileged from the less privileged. Table 8 shows the results for a range of factors ordinarily employed to measure socio-economic privilege. Respondents with higher incomes, those in more prestigious occupations, and those with superior educations were more likely to be knowledgeable than their less privileged counterparts. Even home ownership made for a sizable increase in knowledgeability. This last fact is of special interest. Home ownership differs from the other economic factors in being an index not only of economic privilege but also of family stability and residential permanence. It reflects a certain degree of social commitment and responsibility as well as some degree of integration into the community. On the

Table 8. Knowledge of Trial by Education, Income, Occupation, and Home Ownership

	Education						
	Eighth Grade or Less	Some High School	Finished High School	Business or Trade School	Some College	Finished College	Post-graduate
Per cent knowledgeable[a]	21%	31%	49%	61%	68%	81%	81%
Total number	(119)	(104)	(108)	(18)	(56)	(26)	(27)

	Annual Family Income						
	Under $2,000	$2,000-$3,999	$4,000-$5,000	$6,000-$7,999	$8,000-$9,999	$10,000-$14,999	Above $15,000
Per cent knowledgeable	25%	32%	35%	56%	62%	60%	83%
Total number	(59)	(84)	(105)	(66)	(48)	(42)	(29)

	Occupational Prestige[b]				
	Lower	Lower Middle	Middle	Upper Middle	Upper
Per cent knowledgeable	10%	43%	47%	83%	84%
Total number	(83)	(126)	(122)	(69)	(19)

	Home Ownership	
	Renters	Homeowners
Per cent knowledgeable	32%	53%
Total number	(202)	(255)

[a] The reader should note that in this table a single figure for "per cent knowledgeable" has been substituted for the more cumbersome measure of knowledgeability used in Table 7. "Per cent knowledgeable" refers to the proportion of respondents who answered two or more of the knowledge questions correctly. The residue in each case comprises the unawares and those who knew the answer to only one or to none of the knowledge questions asked. Since the general direction of the results using this measure, is no different from that obtained using the more refined measure, it will be used in the subsequent analysis.

[b] The construction of the measure of occupational prestige is described in Appendix A.

income levels of $6,000 a year and over, the vast majority of the respondents owned their own homes. Nevertheless, renters in this group consistently showed less knowledge of the trial than homeowners despite their equally privileged economic position.[8]

The power of privilege to account for differential involvement in a news event is even more strikingly shown when the various indicators of socio-economic position are considered in combination. A composite index of privilege was constructed by assigning respondents a score based on the number of privileged attributes each possessed. Thus, at one extreme, a score of four was assigned to those who had a high school education or better, had a prestigious occupation (Level 4 or 5; see Appendix A), had a family income of $6,000 or more, and owned their own home. Respondents having none of these characteristics were assigned a score of zero. The rest were then scored according to the number of privileged characteristics they had. Thus, the higher the score, the higher the respondent's socio-economic privilege. Table 9

TABLE 9. KNOWLEDGE OF TRIAL BY LEVEL OF SOCIO-ECONOMIC PRIVILEGE

	Index of Socio-economic Privilege				
	Low 0	1	2	3	High 4
White respondents					
Per cent knowledgeable	39%	41%	48%	71%	88%
Number	(36)	(68)	(66)	(58)	(64)
Negro respondents					
Per cent knowledgeable	10%	12%	23%	50%	[a]
Number	(51)	(56)	(22)	(8)	

[a] No Negro respondents scored 4 on the index of socio-economic privilege.

[8] Among whites who earned more than $6,000 annually, 75 per cent of those who owned their own homes scored as knowledgeable; 55 per cent of renters scored as knowledgeable. While there were relatively few Negroes who earned more than $6,000, the owners nevertheless were more likely to be knowledgeable (21 per cent) than the renters (9 per cent).

sums up the cumulative effects of socio-economic privilege on knowledge. Among white respondents, the proportion knowledgeable climbs from a low of 39 per cent to a high of 88 per cent as socio-economic privilege scores rise from 0 to 4.

It should be emphasized that the effect of socio-economic privilege is not simply a reflection of the better education enjoyed by those better off economically. That the better educated are more informed about serious news events, including the Eichmann trial, is hardly astonishing: Education should result in increased literacy, and increased literacy should result in better comprehension. But privilege—as embodied in occupation and income—has an effect on knowledgeability over and above the influence of education. Not only education, but advantage per se increases knowledgeability.

Table 9 also shows that at every level of privilege for which it was possible to compare Negroes and whites, Negroes were much less knowledgeable than whites. Among the most disprivileged Negro respondents only 10 per cent were knowledgeable (compared to 39 per cent of the most disprivileged whites). Among the most privileged Negroes (score 3) only 50 per cent were knowledgeable (compared to 71 per cent among similarly scored whites). One mechanism by which the disprivileged remain ignorant while the privileged acquire knowledge should be noted. Table 9 shows that not a single Negro had a score of 4 on the index of socio-economic privilege and only eight, or about 6 per cent of the Negro sample, could be scored 3. Sheerly on statistical grounds, the likelihood that a disprivileged Negro comes into contact with a well-educated, well-informed Negro is minimal. Similarly, the relatively well-educated Negro has only a small pool of equally well-educated Negroes upon whom to draw for information and intellectual stimulation.

Among whites, on the other hand, about 42 per cent were

scored 3 or 4 on the index of socio-economic privilege. Thus in the white community, frequent contact both with and among relatively well-educated and well-informed whites is at least possible. Disprivilege thus operates at two levels. Being disprivileged on the grounds of race, Negroes have virtually no opportunity to communicate with whites in general and with well-educated and knowledgeable whites in particular. But the less well-educated and knowledgeable Negro has almost as little opportunity to communicate with well-educated and knowledgeable Negroes, not only because of social class barriers within the Negro community itself but simply because there are so few privileged Negroes with whom to communicate.

Turning to another indicator of privilege—sex—the results confirm our expectations about the operation of privilege. Fifty-two per cent of the men scored as knowledgeable as compared to 37 per cent of the women, a difference of 15 per cent. When this factor is added to the index of socio-economic privilege (by raising the men's privilege score by 1), the effect is to strengthen still further the relation between privilege and knowledgeability (Table 10). At the

TABLE 10. KNOWLEDGE OF TRIAL BY GENERAL LEVEL OF PRIVILEGE

	General Level of Privilege					
	Low 0	1	2	3	4	High 5
White respondents						
Per cent knowledgeable	26%	40%	43%	65%	80%	91%
Number	(19)	(62)	(61)	(54)	(64)	(32)
Negro respondents						
Per cent knowledgeable	0%	17%	17%	28%	50%	[a]
Number	(30)	(54)	(36)	(14)	(4)	

[a] No Negro respondents scored 5.

upper extreme, 91 per cent of the most privileged whites are knowledgeable. Among both Negroes and whites increases in privilege are associated with increments in knowledge.

The relation between age and involvement in public affairs has been shown in past research to be curvilinear: The extremely old and the extremely young exhibit less involvement than intermediate age groups. In terms of the theory of privilege, the very young and the elderly have less access to society, and for this reason they tend to take less interest in public affairs than other age groups.

As Table 11 shows, the very young and the very old are the

TABLE 11. KNOWLEDGE OF TRIAL BY AGE

	Age						
	16–19	20–29	30–39	40–49	50–59	60–69	70+
White respondents							
Per cent knowledgeable	38%	67%	74%	57%	58%	58%	45%
Number	(16)	(39)	(38)	(60)	(65)	(33)	(44)
Negro respondents							
Per cent knowledgeable	0%	17%	18%	19%	17%	0%	0%
Number	(6)	(23)	(34)	(37)	(24)	(9)	(7)

least informed of the seven age groups. The same pattern prevails among Negroes as among whites even though, at every age level, Negroes are much less apt to be knowledgeable than whites.

Since there are so few people in the age extremes, little would be added to the explanatory power of the general privilege index by adding the factor of age to the privilege scores. However, a few words might be said regarding the relatively low levels of knowledge exhibited by the whites aged 40 to 69. People of this age, as well as those 70 and over, were adults or young adults during the 1940s when the worst Nazi persecutions occurred. Yet they show lower levels of knowledge than the 20 to 39 age groups. Living at the time of the historical experience does not seem to have played a significant role in increasing knowledge or involvement in the Eichmann trial.

The results amply demonstrate that involvement in the trial, as measured by being knowledgeable about it, was largely a reflection of the degree of privilege which individuals enjoyed in the community. As Table 10 dramatically shows, when socio-economic privilege, sex, and race are all taken into consideration, knowledgeability concerning the Eichmann trial varies directly with privilege score, ranging from 0 per cent to 91 per cent.

Knowledge and Anti-Semitism

The power of privilege to predict knowledge and involvement is very great, but it is not absolute. Some people with high privilege scores avoided the trial, while others with low privilege scores became knowledgeable about it. Most people gave or withheld attention for the same reasons that normally induce them to read or not to read about any serious news event. However, for a few respondents, the trial apparently stood out, in some way, as a special rather than an ordinary news event.

One aspect of the trial might have invested it with special significance: its particular relevance to anti-Semitism. Some of the testimony was devoted to establishing Eichmann's personal complicity, but a good deal more was spent on exposing the extent and heinousness of the crimes with which he was connected. The trial was, at least in part, a protracted lesson, aimed at all non-Jews, to remind them of the horrors to which acquiescence in anti-Semitism can lead.

Implicit in the proceedings was the hope that those with ambivalent or antagonistic feelings toward Jews would attend to the trial and profit from its message. Before considering whether it actually did win acceptance among those with anti-Semitic tendencies, it is necessary to ask whether the anti-Semite paid enough attention to the trial to learn something about it. Many studies in the past have demonstrated an almost natural tendency for people to avoid coming into contact with anything that runs counter to their prejudices. In a review of research on the reactions of prejudiced people to anti-prejudice propaganda, Cooper and Jahoda found that the prejudiced person typically avoids, distorts, or misunderstands ideas that contradict his own beliefs. The authors concluded that people generally " . . . prefer not to face the implications of ideas opposed to their own so that they do not have to be forced either to defend themselves or to admit error. What they do is to evade the issue psychologically by simply not *understanding the message*."[9] It is conceivable, however, that the Eichmann trial was a powerful enough stimulus to overcome these tendencies.

In order to see whether the Eichmann trial was an exception to the general tendency, comparisons were made of the extent to which people with varying inclinations toward anti-Semitism exposed themselves to the trial. Anti-Semitism was measured in three ways, each index providing a different but related way of evaluating the extent of anti-Semitism.[10] The first or general anti-Semitism index was based on the extent to which a respondent agreed or disagreed with a set of three negative statements about Jews.[11] Each respondent was

[9] Eunice Cooper and Marie Jahoda, "The Evasion of Propaganda: How Prejudiced People Respond to Anti-prejudice Propaganda," *Journal of Psychology*, January 1947, pp. 15–25. Also see Leon Festinger, *A Theory of Cognitive Dissonance* (Stanford: Stanford University Press, 1957), chaps. 6 and 7.

[10] The construction of the anti-Semitism scores is described in Appendix A.

[11] The three statements were: (1) Anyone who employs many people should be careful not to hire a large percentage of Jews. (2) Jews don't like to mix with other people so they would rather live in special areas of their own. (3) The trouble with letting Jews into a nice neighborhood is that they gradually give it a typically Jewish atmosphere. Correlations between pairs

assigned one point for each agreement; hence, higher scores indicate greater anti-Semitism. Agreement with a negative belief does not necessarily imply that the individual harbors negative feelings toward Jews. However, it can be safely assumed that, for most people, negative stereotypes are in fact accompanied by negative feelings, varying in intensity from individual to individual.

Unfavorable beliefs and attitudes may or may not be acted out in discriminatory behavior. A second measure—the discrimination index—gave explicit attention to the discriminatory component in anti-Semitism. It was based on a series of questions asking respondents whether or not they would countenance discriminatory acts against Jews with respect to granting them access to vacation resorts, to employment, and to political office. This measure produced three classes of respondents: those who totally rejected discrimination, those who accepted one or more forms of discrimination, and those who were not sure how they might feel or would act.

A third measure—the self-segregation index—gave recognition to the fact that anti-Semitism may be expressed as an effort to avoid relations with Jews. This measure—actually a broadly conceived measure of the person's disposition to avoid anyone different from him—classified respondents according to the degree to which they would segregate themselves from others on racial, religious, or ethnic grounds. For present purposes, only the simple distinction between those who would segregate themselves from Jews and those who would not is used.

The results indicate that a majority—though sometimes a small one—showed no evidence of anti-Semitism on the particular indices used. On the general anti-Semitism index, 56

---

of beliefs were 0.70 or better. The use of these three indicators was based on a factor analysis of a larger number of items (see Appendix A). Validation of the general anti-Semitism index is presented in Appendix B.

per cent of the sample received a score of zero; they answered all items in a favorable way. Of the remainder, 24 per cent gave an anti-Semitic response on one item; 13 per cent did so on two; only 7 per cent did so on all three. On the discrimination measure, about half—232 persons—totally rejected discriminatory behavior. Somewhat less than a quarter approved of one or more forms of discrimination. Somewhat more than a quarter are unsure of what they would do or how they feel with regard to one or more discriminatory acts. On the self-segregation index, 208 would not object to Jews marrying into their immediate family; 201 respondents would not like it; 49 had no opinion.

It must be emphasized that these are "relative," not "absolute," measures of anti-Semitism. They make it possible to compare in a rough way less and more anti-Semitic individuals, but they do not permit a description of the absolute level of anti-Semitism. The observation that a slight majority manifested no evidence of anti-Semitism must be interpreted solely in terms of the particular measure used. Using other measures, a larger or smaller proportion of the population would score as anti-Semitic. For example, among those who scored zero on the general anti-Semitism index, 23 per cent believed that "one trouble with Jewish businessmen is that they stick together and connive, so that a Gentile doesn't have a fair chance in competition." Had this item been included in the general anti-Semitism index, it would not have been possible to say that a majority of Oaklanders showed no signs of anti-Semitism.

Similar caution must be exercised in describing the other half of the Oakland population as anti-Semitic. One negative belief about Jews does not make a person an anti-Semite. Nevertheless, as Appendix Table B-1 shows, a high correlation exists between an individual's score on the three beliefs included in the general anti-Semitism index and his tendency both to hold other negative beliefs about Jews and to fail to oppose all forms of discrimination.

Because it was found that the general anti-Semitism index predicts other forms of anti-Semitism, it is used throughout the following analysis as the primary measure of anti-Semitism (or, more accurately perhaps, of a proclivity toward anti-Semitism). No matter what measure of anti-Semitism is used, however, a respondent's score is related to his degree of involvement in the Eichmann trial. In every instance those with the greater proclivity toward anti-Semitism showed less knowledge of the trial (Table 12). Among those with scores

TABLE 12. KNOWLEDGE OF TRIAL BY DEGREE OF ANTI-SEMITISM[a]

	General Anti-Semitism Index			
	None 0	Low 1	Medium 2	High 3
Per cent knowledgeable	57%	40%	40%	15%
Number	(213)	(92)	(50)	(27)

	Discrimination Index		
	Reject Discrimination	Unsure	Accept Discrimination
Per cent knowledgeable	55%	36%	28%
Number	(232)	(126)	(100)

	Self-Segregation Index	
	Accept Jews	Reject Jews
Per cent knowledgeable	52%	39%
Number	(208)	(201)

[a] Because information was lacking, it was not possible to score all respondents on two of the measures of anti-Semitism. Seventy-six respondents could not be scored on the general anti-Semitism scale, and 49 on the self-segregation index. The proportion scoring as knowledgeable among these residual groups is 26 per cent and 31 per cent, respectively.

of zero on the general anti-Semitism scale, 57 per cent were knowledgeable about the trial. With increasing evidence of anti-Semitism, the proportion knowledgeable about the trial goes down to 40 per cent and 15 per cent. Among those who would not countenance discrimination, 55 per cent were knowledgeable. Among those who were unsure or who definitely accepted discrimination, 36 per cent and 28 per cent scored as knowledgeable. On the self-segregation index, there is a difference in knowledgeability of 13 percentage points favoring those who would accept a Jew into their family.[12]

These results suggest that the trial did not overcome the usual tendency of people to avoid information that promises to threaten their beliefs and values. However, what is apparent may not in fact be real.

In line with the finding that degree of privilege is an extremely powerful predictor of knowledgeability, it is entirely possible that the more anti-Semitic respondents were relatively uniformed about the trial not because of their attitudes toward Jews but because they tended to be the most disprivileged members of the population. Evidence from past research suggests that those at lower socio-economic levels are more likely to be prejudiced, or at least to verbalize their prejudices, than those on higher socio-economic levels.[13] The

[12] The fact that all three measures of anti-Semitism are related to knowledgeability has implications for the well-known problem of "acquiescence." It has been frequently noted that, when index items are couched in positive terms, unsophisticated respondents can receive high scores simply because they have a tendency to agree to any statement presented to them in an interview. All three beliefs in the general anti-Semitism index were phrased so that a "yes" response would be scored as an anti-Semitic response. Undoubtedly, some who scored high on the general index did so out of acquiescence. Moreover, these are very likely to be the same unsophisticated respondents who scored as not knowedgeable. However, neither the discrimination items nor the self-segregation items were phrased so that a simple "yes" or "no" response was the appropriate answer. Nevertheless, these two measures are also related to knowledgeability.

[13] There have been remarkably few attempts to study the sources of anti-Semitism using nationally representative samples. Stember's analysis of data collected by major polling agencies over a fifteen-year period comes closest to a nationwide appraisal of the social correlates of anti-Semitism. Although his findings suggest that the more educated may tend to hold certain kinds

present data do indicate that in Oakland anti-Semitism tends to be concentrated more heavily among the less privileged.[14] Among both Negroes and whites, those who are more privileged exhibit less anti-Semitism on all three measures. The results shown in Table 13 for the general anti-Semitism index

TABLE 13. ANTI-SEMITISM BY LEVEL OF PRIVILEGE

	General Level of Privilege						
	Low 0	1	2	3	4	High 5	*Total*
White respondents							
Per cent giving anti-Semitic reply[a]	77%	59%	45%	39%	25%	30%	42%
Number	(13)	(51)	(56)	(49)	(57)	(30)	(256)
Negro respondents							
Per cent giving anti-Semitic reply[a]	58%	51%	44%	38%	[b]	[c]	47%
Number	(19)	(37)	(32)	(13)	(3)		(104)

[a] In this and subsequent tables, those who scored 1, 2, or 3 on the general anti-Semitism index are counted as being anti-Semitic. The same relative results are obtained whatever cutting point is used.

[b] There are too few cases on which to base a percentage.

[c] No Negro scored 5.

illustrate the direction of the findings. The lower the privilege score among both Negroes and whites, the greater the tendency to give one or more anti-Semitic responses. This strongly suggests that the relation between anti-Semitism and knowledgeability may be a function of social privilege.

Further analysis shows, however, that anti-Semitism did have an independent effect on knowledgeability. When the relation between anti-Semitism and knowledgeability is examined among those at the same level of privilege, anti-

of negative stereotypes about Jews, on the whole education is associated with attitudes of tolerance [Charles Herbert Stember, *Education and Attitude Change* (New York: Institute of Human Relations Press, 1961)].

[14] See Appendix B for an analysis of the social correlates of anti-Semitism in the Oakland sample.

Semitism continues to be associated with less knowledge of the trial (Table 14). At each level of privilege, those who

TABLE 14. KNOWLEDGE OF TRIAL BY ANTI-SEMITISM AND PRIVILEGE

	General Level of Privilege[a]		
	Low	Medium	High
White respondents			
Per cent knowledgeable among the anti-Semitic	35%	50%	74%
Number	(40)	(44)	(23)
Per cent knowledgeable among the nonanti-Semitic	54%	57%	88%
Number	(24)	(61)	(64)
Negro respondents			
Per cent knowledgeable among the anti-Semitic	3%	16%	[b]
Number	(30)	(19)	
Per cent knowledgeable among the nonanti-Semitic	19%	23%	[c]
Number	(26)	(26)	(3)

[a] In this and subsequent tables, low privilege is defined as a score of 0 or 1 on the privilege index; medium privilege, as a score of 2 or 3; and high privilege, as a score of 4 or 5.

[b] No cases in this cell.

[c] Too few cases on which to base a percentage.

gave anti-Semitic responses on the general anti-Semitism index were less likely to be knowledgeable about the trial than those who gave no anti-Semitic responses.

Comparisons across the rows of Table 14 confirm the earlier findings that knowledgeability is highly related to social privilege. For example, in the first row, which gives the results for whites scored as anti-Semitic, knowledge goes from 35 per cent to 50 per cent to 74 per cent as privilege goes up. All the row percentages indicate that whether or not a person scores as anti-Semitic, the higher his privilege level, the more likely he is to be knowledgeable about the trial. However, the column percentages reveal that at each level of privilege those with anti-Semitic leanings are less likely to be knowledgeable than those who give no anti-Semitic responses.

Further analysis reveals that the anti-Semitically inclined individual exhibits a somewhat greater tendency than others to be unaware of serious news events, whatever his level of privilege. However, even when a person with anti-Semitic tendencies was aware of such events as the Freedom Riders or the tractors-for-rebels exchange, thus indicating some concern for serious news events, he was still less likely than others on the same privilege level to be informed of the details of the Eichmann trial.[15]

Privilege obviously is a more powerful predictor of knowledge than anti-Semitism; at no point does anti-Semitism transcend the relation of privilege to knowledge. The upper-class individual who was anti-Semitic still tended very strongly to be acquainted with the details of the trial. Similarly, even when he was free from prejudice, the less privileged person tended to know less about the trial than the more privileged person. The conclusion that the trial tended to involve those who regularly pay attention to serious news events is thus sustained. However, to the extent that the trial was selective in reaching its audience, it tended to involve most frequently those least inclined to be prejudiced against Jews.

Knowledgeability and Media Exposure

The kinds of people who were least likely to be interested and informed about the Eichmann trial tended to be people

[15] For example, among those who were aware of the tractor-for-rebels exchange, 44 per cent of the low-privileged whites who were anti-Semitic scored as knowledgeable. The equivalent figure for the nonanti-Semitic was 59 per cent. At the highest privilege level, the corresponding figures were 77 per cent and 88 per cent. This propensity for the anti-Semitic to be less knowledgeable about the Eichmann trial manifested itself at all privilege levels among both whites and Negroes.

who are generally uninformed about serious news events, who are socially disprivileged, or who are relatively intolerant of Jews. Nothwithstanding these findings, it may seem astonishing that these persons could have escaped even an elementary knowledge of the circumstances surrounding the trial. For well over a year the trial received extensive coverage in all the mass media: radio, newspapers, television, magazines. There was the additional possibility of learning something about the trial through informal channels of communication, such as talking with friends or associates. How a sizable group could have remained uninformed in the midst of a veritable deluge of information may still be difficult to comprehend.

A partial answer can be found in the different ways in which people exposed themselves to the media of communication. In an effort to assess respondents' exposure to the various media, and the relative success of these media in transmitting information, respondents were asked which of the major media had been a source of information about the trial. The frequencies with which the various media were named are as follows: newspaper reports, 78 per cent; television news reports, 68 per cent; radio, 65 per cent; conversation, 41 per cent; magazines, 36 per cent; special telecasts, 25 per cent. Table 15 shows that this rank order is the same for both the knowledgeable and the unknowledgeable. In large measure, this rank order merely reflects the amount of coverage given by the various media to the trial. However, as will be seen, there is also some evidence to suggest that certain of the media were more effective than others in communicating information about the trial.

The last column in Table 15 shows that the knowledgeable were more likely than the unknowledgeable to mention each medium of communication as a source of information. Whatever the medium, more of the knowledgeable than the unknowledgeable had been exposed to the Eichmann trial through it.

Stated in somewhat different terms, Table 15 shows that the knowledgeable respondents obtained their information from a wider variety of sources than the unknowledgeable.

TABLE 15. SOURCES OF INFORMATION ABOUT THE TRIAL AMONG THE MORE AND THE LESS KNOWLEDGEABLE[a]

	Per Cent Reporting Exposure to Each Medium		
	Knowledgeable	Not Knowledgeable	Percentage Point Difference
Reading a newspaper	91%	72%	19%
Watching television	68	68	0
Hearing about trial on the radio	68	63	5
Talking with someone	50	36	14
Reading a magazine	49	29	20
Seeing a special TV program	30	22	8
Number	(124)	(260)	

[a] In this and all subsequent tables, knowledgeable respondents are those who answered at least three of the four knowledge questions correctly. Unknowledgeable respondents are those who answered no more than two of the questions correctly. Whatever cutting point is used on knowledgeability, the same relative results apply.

This can be shown by calculating the average number of sources mentioned by each group. Those knowledgeable about the trial reported an average of 5.1 sources; those unknowledgeable reported an average of 3.0.

Table 16 reorders the findings reported in the last column of Table 15 and shows that what most distinguishes the

TABLE 16. DIFFERENCES IN MEDIA EXPOSURE OF THE MORE AND THE LESS KNOWLEDGEABLE

	Percentage Point Difference in Exposure— Knowledgeable Less Unknowledgeable
Reading magazine	20
Reading newspaper	19
Talking with someone	14
Seeing special TV program	8
Hearing about trial on the radio	5
Watching television	0

knowledgeable from the unknowledgeable is the tendency of the former to rely on the written word, rather than the broadcast media, as a source of information. This finding suggests that the printed media, which reported the trial in greater detail, were more successful than the truncated news reports of the broadcast media in transmitting information to their audience. One reason the knowledgeable were informed was that they were more likely than the unknowledgeable to read the printed media.

It is safe to assume that the tendency to read the printed media is greater among the privileged than among the disprivileged. In the case of the Eichmann trial, those with lower privilege scores were about as likely to get their information from television as from newspapers. The privileged, in contrast, were much more likely to rely on newspapers than on television. Thus it would appear that the primary road from privilege to detailed knowledge about public issues is via the printed media, which generally provide the most continuous and complete reporting about news events. Not only are the privileged more interested in serious news events, they also turn to the most intensive sources of information. Together these factors help to explain why the more privileged groups exhibited relatively high rates of knowledge about the Eichmann trial and the less privileged had little detailed information.

Summary and Conclusions

The hopes that the public would appreciate the singular importance of the Eichmann trial and that the trial would command extraordinary public attention were not, it is now evident, realized. While the vast majority of the public knew that the trial was taking place, a disappointingly small number were sufficiently interested or sophisticated to gain even the most elementary knowledge about the proceedings. The people who did become involved and knowledgeable were by and large the same people who attend to serious news as a matter of routine and who are interested and literate enough to get their information from the printed rather than only the broadcast media.

Anti-Semites tend in general to pay less attention to serious news events. As a consequence, the Eichmann trial did not reach the anti-Semitic segments of the population to the same degree that it reached the tolerant ones. Over and above this, anti-Semites showed some tendency to avoid becoming informed about the trial even when they were aware of other serious news events. However, it must be remembered that at equal levels of privilege (including education), the anti-Semite probably tends to be less intellectually and culturally sophisticated than his more tolerant counterpart. It is difficult to say, therefore, whether the anti-Semite knew less about the trial because his prejudice intervened or because his relative lack of sophistication stood in the way. Moreover, the level of knowledgeability among the anti-Semitically inclined was not drastically lower than among the tolerant; in view of the demonstrated resistance of people to information that threatens their basic attitudes, it would not be farfetched to conclude that the trial was remarkably effective in getting a body of threatening facts across to the anti-Semitically inclined. However, another conclusion is possible, to which later analysis gives some support. This is that the anti-Semitically inclined attended to the trial as well as they did because they saw no connection between it and their own intolerant attitudes.

It must be emphasized that, while the Eichmann trial may not have been singled out for special attention, it probably received no less attention than the general gamut of serious news events. The bulk of the public, for all the lip service it pays to the desirability of being interested and well-informed about public affairs, is neither. The responsibility is relegated, however unconsciously, to a small minority for whom being informed is at once a sign of their status and a means of retaining it. For the most part, the majority is willing to have it this way, and to become deeply involved only when public issues are personally relevant. Several writers have advanced the view that some measure of political apathy is desirable—that a democracy would not work if every issue always engaged every element of the body politic. Universal participation, according to this view, would generate deep cleavages in society, and might thereby hinder or even preclude the solution of problems through democratic means.[16]

However valid this view may be with reference to the preservation of democratic institutions, it may not apply to a certain class of moral issues among which anti-Semitism and prejudice stand out. Without wide-scale and explicit rejection of anti-Semitism, the danger of a repetition of the Nazi horrors remains a persistent one. From this perspective, the failure of so large a stimulus as the Eichmann trial to penetrate the public's consciousness is significant.

Of greater significance are the kinds of attitudes and opinions it generated among those who followed the proceedings. This seems to be of paramount importance and is the major concern of the remainder of this book.

[16] For example, the authors of the Elmira voting study argue that political apathy has both negative and positive functions for society. On the one hand, apathetic conformity endangers the preservation of democratic institutions. On the other hand, "the apathetic segment of America probably has helped to hold the system together and cushioned the shock of disagreement, adjustment, and change" [Bernard R. Berelson, Paul F. Lazarsfeld, and William N. McPhee, *Voting* (Chicago: University of Chicago Press, 1955), p. 322].

CHAPTER 3

EICHMANN'S COMPLICITY AND GUILT

KNOWLEDGE and information should precede holding an opinion, but this principle is seldom reflected in reality. People have opinions on all sorts of issues about which they know practically nothing. While a few people will answer a question by saying they have no opinion about it, the vast majority, informed or uninformed, have opinions to express. Opinions on the Eichmann trial were no exception to the rule.

In exploring these opinions, what has already been learned about knowledge is relevant. The following analysis demonstrates that the individual's knowledgeability concerning the details of the trial made a considerable difference in how he responded to the various trial issues. Knowledge was not always decisive, nor was it the sole factor, but the informed tended to respond differently from the uninformed, and to do so in a fairly systematic and consistent way.

Three questions are explored: Who accepted and who rejected the prosecution's case against Eichmann? Who viewed the trial as legal and who saw it as illegal? Who approved of the death penalty for Eichmann and who did not? These questions are considered in turn, in this and the succeeding two chapters. How responses influenced receptivity to the trial's ultimate educational ends is analyzed in Chapter 6.

The Case for the Prosecution and the Defense

In one respect the informed and the uninformed were in a similar position regarding the trial: Both had to rely upon the mass media for forming impressions and coming to conclusions. On the question of Eichmann's guilt, the mass media reported extensively the cases of both the prosecution and the defense. In terms of sheer amount of space, however, the public was considerably more exposed to arguments for Eichmann's guilt than for his innocence. Not only did the prosecution take longer to present its case, but editorial opinion was almost universally on the side of the prosecution. Editorials in the Oakland area did not even voice the legalistic argument, sometimes advanced in other parts of America, that Eichmann should be presumed innocent prior to the outcome of the trial. It was taken for granted that Eichmann had long ago been proved guilty and that the trial, though justified and scrupulously conducted, was a mere formality.

The only grounds that the mass media presented for concluding that Eichmann was not guilty was their reporting of Eichmann's defense. But even here no attempt was made to deny that Eichmann had helped to administer and facilitate the mass murder of European Jews during World War II. The defense did attempt to minimize Eichmann's role, arguing that he had merely followed orders he was morally and legally bound to obey. It did deny that Eichmann had participated in decision-making and that he had personally engaged in murder. But it did not deny that Eichmann had actually done many of the things he was accused of. The defense was legal rather than factual. Its argument was that, while Eichmann had perhaps participated in a moral crime out of an excess of loyalty and subservience, he had not, strictly speaking, committed a legal crime.

Unless one looked to the anti-Semitic "hate" press, there were no grounds for concluding that Eichmann was innocent. Displaying once again its unique capacity for logical ingenuity, the racist press spoke up for the innocence of the man in the dock. The accused, it said, is not Eichmann at all, but a willing sacrificial goat serving the propaganda aims of Israel. Or, if he really is Eichmann, he is innocent, since no mass murder of Jews ever occurred. It is true, of course, that Jews were murdered, but they were murdered not as Jews but as enemies of the German Reich—and in any case the figures have been grossly exaggerated.[1] These views were never presented in the responsible mass media and were not salient considerations for most people in forming their opinions of Eichmann's guilt or innocence. In the Oakland sample, there was little or no indication that respondents were even aware of the involuted arguments of the anti-Semitic press on behalf of Eichmann's innocence.

Anyone who paid close attention to press reports of the trial would also have become acquainted with the many arguments for Eichmann's guilt presented by the prosecution. One argument, offered rather halfheartedly, was that Eichmann had personally killed a young Jewish boy for allegedly stealing some cherries from Eichmann's garden in Budapest. A second reason, offered much more compellingly, was that Eichmann was far from being the underling that he and his attorney portrayed him to be. The efficiency and initiative he had displayed in performing his tasks, it was argued, could have been inspired only by zeal and enthusiasm for Nazi policy. Moreover, behind Eichmann was a long history of convinced, ideological anti-Semitism. Finally, there was

[1] For an analysis of demagogic techniques and appeals, see *Prophets of Deceit* (New York: Harper & Row, 1940) by Leo Lowenthal and Norbert Guterman. The incredible interpretations and the senseless and contradictory statements promulgated by the racist press with regard to the Eichmann trial are generally characteristic of anti-Semitic speeches and writings.

ample evidence that he had actively participated in making decisions and formulating policy.

Any of these reasons, it was asserted, warranted a verdict of guilty. But even if these were rejected, and Eichmann's own assertions accepted, no ground for acquittal existed. In rejecting Eichmann's claim that he had served merely as a lackey for his superiors, the prosecution was careful to note that, even if accurate, Eichmann's self-portrayal would not be a valid defense for the crimes committed. On the contrary, subordinates are responsible for crimes against humanity even when ordered to commit them by their superiors.

On every side, then, the public was surrounded with arguments and evidence for Eichmann's guilt. Careful readers, however, might have encountered some of the controversy that centered around the picture of Eichmann being painted by the prosecution. Observers were not uniformly convinced that it was in the long-range interest of the struggle against anti-Semitism to portray Eichmann as a sadistic monster who had personally murdered. The more the prosecution portrayed Eichmann as a monster and criminal, it was argued, the less fitting he became as a symbol of the ordinary, everyday anti-Semite who helped to create Nazism and who, while not an active participant, certainly condoned the barbaric murder of the Jews. The prosecution's picture of Eichmann would permit the "respectable" anti-Semite to disassociate himself from Eichmann and thereby reject responsibility for the consequences of his own anti-Semitism.[2]

[2] Before the trial, one writer commented: "The trial will make it, if anything, easier for the shouting mothers in Louisiana or the parading students in Georgia to believe that what they did has nothing to do with the horrors of Auschwitz. Nor will the decent citizens all over our country who guard their clubs from Jewish members see any connection. Not even the Louisiana mothers, to say nothing of the more gentlemanly segregationists, have probably ever harmed another citizen's hair. What connection could there be with the butchers of Auschwitz?" The author's opinion was that, "to make us believe that the destruction of 6,000,000 Jews can be understood by talk-

Furthermore, some observers feared that, by portraying Eichmann as an extraordinarily degenerate person who had himself personally murdered, the prosecution was inadvertently seeming to lay the crimes against the Jews at the feet of a single individual, rather than directing responsibility toward the Nazi party, the German people, and the world at large. It was held that by arguing the case as it did, the prosecution ran the danger of winning easy assent to Eichmann's guilt, even from the anti-Semite, and of encouraging the world to expiate its guilt through Eichmann's conviction.

While the prosecution did introduce evidence that Eichmann had killed a Jewish boy in his Budapest garden, its case rested primarily upon Eichmann's ideological anti-Semitism and his active participation in the mass murder of the Jews. But even this picture of Eichmann was attacked, at least in the more sophisticated media. Indeed the question is still being debated as to whether Eichmann should not be conceived of as a passionless robot rather than an enthusiastic and zealous ideologue. According to one interpretation, totalitarianism is characterized precisely by its capacity to turn individuals into robots who perform evil in a perfectly routine and emotionless manner.[3] Such a view argues that Eichmann's particular crime was subservience rather than

---

ing to one depraved underling is both impossible and a mistake. . . . The trial will not make it easier for us to realize that, however remotely, we all share in this moral catastrophe . . ." (Hans Zeisel, "Who Are the Guilty?" *Saturday Review*, April 8, 1961).

[3] According to Hannah Arendt, totalitarianism strives for total domination of social life and, ultimately, for the transformation of human nature itself. This is possible "only if each and every person can be reduced to a never changing identity of reactions, so that each of these bundles can be exchanged for any other." The Nazi concentration camps, she argues, were intended both as laboratories where the individuality and spontaneity of their victims were systematically destroyed and as training grounds where normal men—the SS guard—were taught to participate unemotionally in mass murders and unspeakable perversions [*The Origins of Totalitarianism* (NewYork: Meridian Books, 1960), pp. 437–459].

enthusiasm. While the trial was still going on, a number of writers expressed a somewhat different interpretation of Nazism—that, far from creating submissive obedience, Nazism was a product of tendencies toward obedience long present in German culture.[4] But the upshot of their criticism was the same: that to insist on Eichmann as a leader and an unusually vicious anti-Semite was to destroy his value as a symbol of the servile acquiescence to authority that made the Nazi barbarities possible.

It is difficult to say how much criticism of the prosecution's picture of Eichmann entailed explicit rejection of the evidence. One highly responsible French journalist, sympathetic to the trial and its purposes, did argue that his own examination of the facts revealed Eichmann to be precisely the sort of person the defense said he was.[5] Most criticism, however, ignored the evidence and seemed to be based on the feeling that, no matter what the actual truth about Eichmann's complicity was, a profounder and more subtle lesson would have emerged from the trial had Eichmann been portrayed as a mere cog in the Nazi machine. In this case, assent to his guilt might have been less widespread, but it would have represented deeper conviction and understanding.

For its part, the prosecution did present evidence that pointed to Eichmann's active participation in the "final solution" and even to an individual act of murder. There is no reason to suppose that, in light of the facts, the prosecution could have pursued its case other than as it did. To what extent the public would have accepted the verdict of guilty had Eichmann been portrayed as nothing more than a spineless underling is another question, however, and one soon to be considered.

In any case, it was altogether possible to agree that Eich-

[4] This view was early expressed in Erich Fromm, *Escape From Freedom* (New York: Rinehart, 1941), especially Chap. 6.

[5] François Bondy, "On Misunderstanding Eichmann," *Encounter*, November 1961, pp. 32–37.

mann was guilty and yet have different interpretations of his crimes and the nature of his guilt. The public was overwhelmingly exposed to opinion and evidence that he was guilty, but it could also have been exposed to interpretations of Eichmann's role that differed from the prosecution's. Moreover, it was possible to come to the conclusion that the prosecution's picture of Eichmann was unconvincing quite independently of the reservations sometimes expressed in the elite press.

Public Images of Eichmann

The evidence presented at the trial, and the way this evidence was reported and interpreted in the responsible mass media, offered three images of Eichmann's complicity. One image was that he was a monster—a sadist, a moral degenerate who had personally murdered. A second image was that he was a zealot, probably not personally engaging in murder, but carrying out his assignment with enthusiasm and zeal. A third image was that he was a bureaucrat, an acquiescent cog in the Nazi machine, acting primarily out of obedience and performing his tasks with impersonal efficiency.

Responses to two questions in the interview provided a basis for estimating the distribution of these three images in the sample. One question asked respondents whether they thought Eichmann himself killed any Jews. The other asked how Eichmann had gone about carrying out his orders: Had he done more than ordered, about as much as ordered, or less than ordered? In answer to the first question, 23 per cent agreed that Eichmann had personally murdered, 40 per cent said he had not, and the remaining 37 per cent replied "don't know."[6] On the second question, 52 per cent replied that

[6] Respondents who indicated they were unaware of the trial were not, of course, asked for their opinions on trial issues. Except where otherwise noted, all percentages are now based on the awares only (384 cases).

Eichmann had done more than ordered, 20 per cent that he had done about as much as ordered, 2 per cent that he had done less than ordered; the remaining 26 per cent had no opinion. On the basis of their replies to these two questions, respondents were classified as having the monster, the zealot, or the bureaucrat image of Eichmann.

The monster image: Eichmann personally murdered and did more than his superiors required.
The zealot image: Eichmann did not personally murder but nevertheless did more than his superiors required.
The bureaucrat image: Eichmann did not personally murder and did only as much as ordered.

A handful of people believed that Eichmann had done less than ordered, and these people were said to have a scapegoat image of Eichmann. The seventy respondents who answered "don't know" to both questions were classified as being imageless. Table 17 shows how respondents were classified

TABLE 17. CONSTRUCTION OF IMAGES OF EICHMANN'S COMPLICITY

	Reply to: *"Do You Think That Eichmann Himself Killed Any Jews?"*			
Eichmann's Responsibility	Yes	No	Don't Know	*Total*
Did more than his superiors required	Monster	Zealot	Zealot	
Number	(68)	(86)	(44)	(198)
Did just about as his superiors required	Inconsistent	Bureaucrat	Bureaucrat	
Number	(8)	(40)	(27)	(75)
Don't know	Monster	Bureaucrat	Imageless	
Number	(12)	(20)	(70)	(102)
Did less than his superiors required	Inconsistent	Scapegoat	Scapegoat	
Number	(1)	(5)	(3)	(9)
Total	(89)	(151)	(144)	(384)

when they answered "don't know" to one of the two questions and the basis on which it was decided that nine respondents had inconsistent images.

The distribution of images of Eichmann is shown in Table 18. Of the various images, the one picturing Eichmann as a zealot was selected by a larger proportion of the public than any other. Of the awares, 34 per cent chose the zealot image;

TABLE 18. DISTRIBUTION OF IMAGES OF EICHMANN'S COMPLICITY

Images	Those Who Were Aware of the Trial	Total Sample
Monster	21%	17%
Zealot	34	28
Bureaucrat	23	19
Scapegoat	2	2
Imageless	18	16
Inconsistent	2	2
Unaware of trial		16
Number	(384)	(458)

21 per cent chose the monster image, and 23 per cent saw Eichmann as a bureaucrat. Two per cent saw him as a scapegoat who did less than ordered. Finally, 2 per cent had inconsistent images, while 18 per cent failed to form an image. When the imageless are added to the 16 per cent who remained oblivious of the trial, 32 per cent of the public can be said to have had no conception of the charges against Eichmann (see the second column in Table 18).

The prosecution evidently failed to convince a great majority of the public of its *total* case against Eichmann. Only 21 per cent of the awares agreed that Eichmann had personally killed. However, as was mentioned earlier, the prosecution did not make the murder of the Jewish boy a major element in its case. When this is considered, then 55 per cent of the awares agreed with all or part of the prosecution's case against Eichmann. The 23 per cent who held the bureaucrat image of Eichmann, as well as the 2 per cent who saw him as a scapegoat, remained unconvinced by the prosecution's case, for the image of Eichmann as a bureaucrat was not the image that the prosecution intended to convey nor the grounds on which Eichmann's guilt was being established.

As might be expected, those who saw Eichmann as monster or zealot were overwhelmingly inclined to see him as guilty. Among those who held the monster image, 85 per cent voted him guilty, and 11 per cent elected to express no opinion; among those who held the zealot image, 83 per cent voted him guilty, and 14 per cent had no opinion (Table 19). Considering only those with an opinion, the monster image produced a verdict of guilty in 96 per cent of the cases; the zealot image, in 97 per cent of the cases.

TABLE 19. OPINIONS ON EICHMANN'S GUILT BY IMAGE OF EICHMANN[a]

	Image of Eichmann's Complicity				
Verdict	Monster	Zealot	Bureaucrat	Scapegoat[b]	Imageless
Guilty	85%	83%	61%	(2)	56%
Not guilty	4	3	11	(4)	4
Don't Know	11	14	28	(2)	40
	100%	100%	100%	(8)	100%
Number	(80)	(130)	(87)	(8)	(70)
Of those with an opinion:					
Per cent replying "guilty"	96%	97%	84%		93%
Number	(71)	(112)	(63)		(42)

[a] Those with an inconsistent image are omitted from this table. Of these 9 people, 7 saw Eichmann as guilty; 2 had no opinion.
[b] No percentages are reported for the scapegoat image because of the small number of cases.

An image of Eichmann as a bureaucrat was less likely to produce a verdict of guilty. Not only did fewer people with this image believe in his guilt (only 61 per cent), but more people (28 per cent) refused to express an opinion. Among those who did express an opinion, 84 per cent agreed to his guilt. This constitutes a relative decline in guilty verdicts whichever way the percentages are viewed. It is true that a substantial majority of those with the bureaucrat image came to the conclusion that Eichmann was guilty. Among those with an opinion, an overwhelming majority did so. Nevertheless, the decline in guilty verdicts among those who conceived of Eichmann as a mere subordinate would seem to justify the actual conduct of the trial. It suggests that, had the prosecution brought a mere underling to trial and sought to convince public opinion of his guilt, it would have been less successful in gaining assent to the verdict. Although the decrease in the percentage of not-guilty verdicts among those who held the bureaucrat image was only about 12 points for those who had an opinion, it—together with the substantial increase in "don't know" responses—suggests that a segment of the public would resist holding a subordinate responsible if he were following official orders, and that this segment would increase as the position of the accused became more obscure and unimportant.

Among the various images of Eichmann's complicity, the only one that seems patently hostile to the trial is the scapegoat image. Of the eight people who held this image, that is, believed Eichmann had done less than he was ordered to, four said he was not guilty, two had no opinion, and two felt he was guilty. While the number of cases is small, this image produced the largest proportion of not-guilty verdicts. Though they constituted virtually an infinitesimal proportion, a few people in the general population apparently accepted Eichmann's portrayal of himself as not only a submissive but a reluctant subordinate.

It will be recalled that 18 per cent of the awares were classified as imageless, that is, as having no opinion about the nature of Eichmann's crimes or Eichmann's role. It might be supposed that these people would also have no opinion about his guilt. This was not the case. It is true that substantially more of the imageless had no opinion on his guilt—the figure is 40 per cent—and only a bare majority (56 per cent) decided he was guilty. But the majority did have an opinion, and among them, 93 per cent thought of Eichmann as guilty. Thus, among those with an opinion on guilt, not having an image produced almost as high a proportion of guilty verdicts as the monster or zealot image of Eichmann. This finding suggests that the public was under considerable constraint to agree to Eichmann's guilt, and that this constraint operated even among those who were so little involved in the trial that they had formed no opinion of Eichmann's role and the grounds of his guilt.

The imageless effectively testify to the fact that many people were able to come to a verdict on Eichmann's guilt without a clear picture of the charges against him. But many of those who formed an image of Eichmann's complicity also came to their conclusions on the basis of very little knowledge about the trial or the evidence presented at it. It was earlier reported that at best no more than 33 per cent of the awares could be classified as substantially informed concerning the details of the Eichmann case.[7] Yet 82 per cent formed some image of Eichmann's complicity and 78 per cent came to a judgment on his guilt.

Presumably most of the people who were classified as uninformed on the four-item knowledgeability index were also people who did not follow the proceedings with care and attention. How then did people come to their conceptions of Eichmann and their verdicts of guilt or innocence? Which were informed, which uninformed images? Which seem to have been based on acquaintance with the evidence, which to have been formed in other ways? What role, if any, did anti-Semitism play in the way people imagined Eichmann's complicity and guilt? Since the answers to these questions are quite different for Negro and white citizens of Oakland, it is

[7] Thirty-three per cent of the awares were able to answer more than two of the four knowledge questions correctly.

necessary to consider them separately in the analysis that follows.

The White Community's Response to Eichmann's Role

As has been shown, people are variously equipped to form opinions about any issue. They vary in how much detailed knowledge they have of an issue. They differ in the degree of sophistication with which they can interpret whatever facts they have. Although sophistication and knowledge play an important role in opinion formation, opinion cannot be completely understood in these terms. Idiosyncratic and even unconscious factors, which research may be unable to ferret out, inevitably enter into the decision-making process. Transitory moods as well as more stable and deep-rooted prejudices exert their influence. In addition, when people are questioned by a professional interviewer, as in the present case, their reaction to the interviewer and to the interviewing situation may also significantly shape the opinions they express. Because so many diverse and subtle influences contribute to opinion formation, one cannot hope to comprehend all the factors that led the public to its diverse images of Eichmann. The only feasible goal is an understanding of the major and more measurable factors that entered into their choices.

In undertaking the analysis, it was assumed that rational considerations played some part in people's assessment of the trial, and that amount of knowledge concerning the trial as well as sophistication would be major factors in explaining diverse responses. It was further assumed that the individual's judgment would also be influenced by the kinds of beliefs, attitudes, and feelings he had developed toward Jews. As has already been seen, the extent of his attentiveness to the trial was influenced by such factors. It is reasonable to suppose that they exerted a comparable influence on the way he formed his opinion about the various trial issues.

With regard to the relation between knowledge and image, there are two plausible but contradictory suppositions: (1) that those best informed about the circumstances of the trial would be those most acquainted with the evidence and most convinced by the prosecution's case, while those least informed about the circumstances of the trial would be least acquainted with the evidence and thus least equipped to arrive at an image of Eichmann congruent with that of the prosecution; (2) that being knowledgeable about the evidence might serve to sensitize people to the ambiguities present in the prosecution's case and thus produce skepticism and disagreement.

In order to understand the relation between knowledge and image, it was decided to compare the levels of knowledgeability of six groups of people. Four groups were constructed out of those who saw Eichmann as guilty: those who saw Eichmann as a monster, those who saw him as a zealot, those who saw him as a bureaucrat, and those who were imageless. The small group of seven whites who saw him as a bureaucrat and *not guilty* were separated out as a distinct group.[8] The sixth group consists of the imageless who had no opinion on Eichmann's guilt.[9]

[8] It is recognized that seven cases are scarcely sufficient to warrant analysis. However, this group is important because among the whites they constitute the only persons who were clearly persuaded by Eichmann's defense. Of the five whites with the scapegoat image, only one considered Eichmann not guilty.

[9] To facilitate the presentation, or because there are too few cases, the following groups are omitted from this analysis:

Image	*Verdict*	*Cases*
Monster	Not guilty	0
Monster	No opinion on guilt	8
Zealot	Not guilty	1
Zealot	No opinion on guilt	11
Bureaucrat	No opinion on guilt	14
Scapegoat	All verdicts	5
Imageless	Not guilty	2
Inconsistent	All verdicts	7

The six groups differed markedly in their degree of knowledge about the trial (Table 20). At one extreme 18 per cent scored as knowledgeable; at the other extreme, 86 per cent. The totally opinionless, with no image of Eichmann's role or

TABLE 20. KNOWLEDGEABILITY BY IMAGES OF EICHMANN'S COMPLICITY AND GUILT
(white respondents only)

Image of Eichmann's Complicity	*Verdict*	*Knowledgeable* Per cent	Number
Monster	Guilty	36%	(50)
Zealot	Guilty	38	(82)
Bureaucrat	Guilty	59	(39)
Bureaucrat	Not Guilty	86	(7)
Imageless	Guilty	33	(33)
Imageless	No opinion on guilt	18	(17)

guilt, were as usual the least knowledgeable group. Those who saw Eichmann as monster or as zealot and those who were imageless but gave a verdict of guilty showed approximately equal levels of knowledge. In each case, roughly one-third were knowledgeable. A considerably greater proportion of those with a bureaucrat image were knowledgeable. Among those who saw him as guilty, 59 per cent scored as knowledgeable; among the seven white respondents who saw him as a guiltless subordinate, six, or 86 per cent, were knowledgeable.

The monster and the zealot images were on the whole uninformed images. While these images were sometimes held by well-informed people, generally speaking they attracted people who could have had only scant knowledge of the proceedings. In fact, comparing the imageless with those who held the monster or zealot images, roughly comparable proportions were knowledgeable. The image of Eichmann as a bureaucrat was by far the most informed image. Whether or not they thought that Eichmann should be held responsible, those who saw him as a bureaucrat were generally informed about the trial.

The results indicate that the more a person agreed with the prosecution's case against Eichmann, the greater the likelihood that he was recruited from the ranks of those uninformed about the trial. Conversely the more a person disagreed with the case against Eichmann, the greater was the probability that he came from the ranks of the knowledgeable. Indeed, those who rejected the prosecution's case entirely and saw Eichmann as a guiltless subordinate were the most likely of all to be knowledgeable.[10] This does not mean, it should be emphasized, that most of the public took a critical stand. As was seen earlier, the majority of those with an opinion agreed with the prosecution's case against Eichmann. The majority also agreed that Eichmann was guilty, regardless of their image of Eichmann. However, what resistance there was to the prosecution's case came from those segments of the population who were relatively well-informed about the trial.

That the unconvinced were generally informed, and the convinced generally uninformed, represents something of a paradox. Sixty-four per cent of those who held the monster image were relatively poorly informed and in all probability had never heard of the specific charge that Eichmann had murdered a Jewish boy. Yet, paradoxically, these people agreed that Eichmann had personally murdered. It is possible that those who held the monster image and those who held the zealot and bureaucrat images were all equally aware of the charge, and that the former accepted it while the latter rejected it—but this is not a plausible interpretation. What seems to distinguish the group with the monster

[10] Again, the reader is reminded that this result is based on only seven cases. Nevertheless, the result is consistent with the more general finding that the more a person was critical of the prosecution's case, the greater was the likelihood that he was informed.

image was that they believed Eichmann had personally killed even though they were not aware of evidence supporting that image.

A possible explanation of this paradoxical finding lies in the fact that people were exposed to the trial through the mass media and not through direct access to the trial proceedings themselves. Presumably, those who knew the least about the trial limited themselves to reading the headlines in local newspapers and listening to truncated reports on local radio and television stations. Here Eichmann was often characterized as a murderer. From this many may have concluded that Eichmann had personally killed.

The monster image among the uninformed seems to represent, therefore, not informed acceptance of the prosecution's case, but impressions gained from the rhetoric of the trial as reported in the mass media. Much the same can be said about the uninformed image of Eichmann as zealot. For those whose acquaintance with the trial was minimal, the process of forming an image of Eichmann was largely a matter of discerning the portrait of Eichmann being projected by the mass media. Thus the less knowledgeable the respondent, the more his impressions seemed to coincide with the prosecution's portrayal.

Those who were relatively knowledgeable about the trial were presumably better acquainted than the unknowledgeable with the evidence pertaining to Eichmann's role. Why, then, did a substantial minority reject it? In the first place, they were likely to realize that the charge of personal murder was not a significant aspect of the prosecution's case, and this alone would help to account for the smaller porportion of the informed who held the monster image. They were also more apt to be aware of the questions raised in the more sophisticated journals of opinion about the underlying logic and possibly harmful effects of the prosecution's case. Moreover, some of those who followed the proceedings might simply have remained unconvinced that Eichmann's demeanor in court coincided with the prosecution's portrayal.

Furthermore, some of the more sophisticated might have replied that Eichmann had done no more than follow orders simply because they had a sophisticated image of Nazism. It was remarked earlier that most reservations concerning the trial expressed in the sophisticated media seemed to be based far less on an examination of the evidence than on fears that the Eichmann case as presented would falsify the fundamental realities of the Nazi system. For much the same reason, some of the respondents may have answered as they did in order to avoid any possible implication that the atrocities were traceable to Eichmann as an individual, and were not the deliberate, conscious, and premeditated policy of the Nazi government. Under Nazism, murder was quite literally a routine, a matter of giving and following orders, and it is this fact that some respondents may have wished to convey by their answers. This interpretation suggests a high order of sophistication on the part of some portion of the public. Only 14 per cent of the white awares, however, held the guilty bureaucrat image.

A clearer and more accurate picture of the process by which people came to their images of Eichmann can be gained by considering the joint effects of knowledgeability and sophistication on respondents' images. The measure of sophistication used is the measure of privilege developed in the previous chapter. That index, it will be recalled, was based on the notion that individuals may be distinguished in terms of their involvement in the larger society, which in turn is a function of the degree to which they are given or denied the rewards of that society. The factors that make for involvement or for being privileged—high education, high income, a prestigious occupation, being a male, owning a home—may also be thought of as indicators of how sophisticated a person is. It is recognized that privilege is by no means an infallible indicator of intellectual sophistication. However, in past research, the correlation between privilege and sophistication has been found to be high, so that privilege can be used as a serviceable, if less than perfect, indicator of sophistication.[11]

The following analysis concentrates on the influence of both knowledge and sophistication on images of Eichmann's complicity and guilt. To this end, the white respondents among the awares were divided into four groups: those who scored low on both knowledge and sophistication, those who scored low on knowledge but high on sophistication, those who scored high on knowledge but low on sophistication, and those who scored high on both.[12] For each of these groups it was then determined whether they were more or less likely

[11] A word is in order as to why the concept of sophistication is now being substituted for the concept of privilege when both are based on identical indicators. The reason lies in our desire to avoid the implication that privilege-related or class-related "motives" of an ideological kind inspired the different images of Eichmann. Earlier, in analyzing knowledgeability, it was plausible to suppose that privilege increases the motivation to participate fully in the larger society and thus to gain knowledge of the Eichmann trial as an important news event. But there is no evidence to suggest, at least in the white community, that privilege or lack of privilege in any sense "motivated" the choice of image. More likely, images were influenced by the intellectual and cultural sophistication associated with privilege rather than by privilege-linked motives.

Discussions of the relation between disprivilege and lack of sophistication can be found in Seymour Martin Lipset, "Working Class Authoritarianism," in *Political Man* (Garden City, N.Y.: Doubleday, 1960), pp. 97–130; Martin Trow, "Cultural Sophistication and Higher Education," in *Selection and Educational Differentiation* (Berkeley: University of California Field Service Center and Center for the Study of Higher Education, n.d.), pp. 107–123; Herbert Hyman and Paul Sheatsley, "The Authoritarian Personality—A Methodological Critique," in Richard Christie and Marie Jahoda (eds.), *Studies in the Scope and Method of "The Authoritarian Personality"* (Glencoe, Ill.: The Free Press, 1954), especially pp. 91–96; and Herbert C. Kelman and Janet Barclay, "The F Scale as a Measure of Breadth of Perspective," *Journal of Abnormal and Social Psychology*, 1963, pp. 608–615.

[12] Those who answered three or four of the four knowledge questions correctly were scored as high in knowledge, the remainder as low in knowledge. Those who scored 4 or 5 on the privilege index were scored as high in sophistication, those with lower privilege scores as low in sophistication.

than the average white Oaklander to accept each of the images of Eichmann's complicity and guilt.[13] The procedure used produces scores that range above and below 1. A score of 1 signifies that a group was just as likely as the average Oaklander to select a given image of Eichmann's role. A score of less than 1 indicates that a group "underchose" a particular image, a score of more than 1 that a group "overchose" a given image in relation to the total sample. The reader is reminded that the results for those who chose the image of Eichmann as a legally guiltless bureaucrat are based on a very small number of cases; these results, therefore, must be treated cautiously.

All in all, the results form a highly consistent pattern (Table 21). People of low knowledge and low sophistication, when they had an image, overchose the monster and zealot images. But they favored the former over the latter; the coefficients are 1.15 and 1.03 respectively. At the same time, they avoided the two bureaucrat images, in particular the image of Eichmann as a guiltless bureaucrat. Here, the coefficients are 0.72 for guilty bureaucrat and 0.32 for guiltless bureaucrat. In general, people whose low knowledge was matched by low sophistication tended to accept the prosecution's case against Eichmann.

Low knowledge led people to avoid the two bureaucrat images regardless of sophistication. In fact, the uninformed who were sophisticated were even more prone than their unsophisticated counterparts to avoid the image of Eichmann as guilty bureaucrat; the coefficients are 0.51 for the sophisticated and 0.72 for the unsophisticated. However, sophistication did influence the relative choice between monster and zealot images. Whereas the unsophisticated favored the mon-

[13] This was done by computing the ratio of the actual image choices of the four knowledge-privilege groups to the image choices that would be expected if privilege and knowledge had no influence on choice.

TABLE 21. JOINT EFFECT OF SOPHISTICATION AND KNOWLEDGE ON EICHMANN'S COMPLICITY AND GUILT
(white respondents only)

		Relative Appeal of Different Images of Eichmann's Complicity and Guilt[a]						
Level of Knowledge	*Level of Sophistication*	Monster (guilty)	Zealot (guilty)	Guilty Bureaucrat	Guiltless Bureaucrat	Imageless, Guilty	Imageless, No Opinion	*Total Number*
Low	Low	1.15	1.03	0.72	0.32	0.97	1.38	(98)
Low	High	0.90	1.09	0.51	[b]	1.57	1.30	(35)
High	Low	1.27	0.84	1.41	1.43	0.75	0.32	(46)
High	High	0.49	1.02	1.54	2.86	0.90	0.64	(46)
Number		(50)	(82)	(38)	(7)	(33)	(15)	(225)

[a] Scores above 1 signify that an image of Eichmann's role was overselected by a particular "sophistication-knowledge" group (see note 12 in this chapter). Scores below 1 signify underselection of an image. A score of exactly 1 indicates that the image was as likely to be selected by the group as by the average Oaklander.

[b] No cases in this cell.

ster over the zealot image (1.15 versus 1.03), the sophisticated were more likely to favor the zealot over the monster image (1.09 versus 0.90). Sophistication had little effect on the general propensity of the uninformed to avoid criticism of the prosecution's case. It did, however, inhibit acceptance of Eichmann as a personal murderer.

In contrast to people with low knowledge, those with high knowledge tended to overselect the two bureaucrat images. This was true regardless of level of sophistication, though the sophisticated reveal a greater propensity in this direction than the unsophisticated. The coefficient for the highly sophisticated on the guilty bureaucrat image, for example, is 1.54 as compared to 1.41 for the unsophisticated. As among the low-knowledgeable, sophistication influenced the choice between the monster and zealot images. Again, the sophisticated favored the zealot image (1.02) over the monster image (0.49) whereas the unsophisticated were more disposed toward the monster image (1.27 as contrasted with 0.84).

In sum, introducing the level of sophistication into the analysis does not materially change the earlier finding that it was the more knowledgeable who were the most prone to adopt a critical stance toward the prosecution's case. Sophistication increases criticism by the highly informed. Its more significant effect, however, was not to engender greater criticism but to lead people to reject the idea that Eichmann was a personal murderer.[14]

The finding that it was the sophisticated and informed elements of the Oakland population who rejected the prosecution's case against Eichmann reveals another paradox, besides the one already mentioned. The previous chapter showed that those with anti-Semitic tendencies were gen-

[14] Among the imageless, sophistication had the effect of disposing the unknowledgeable to say that Eichmann was guilty rather than to have no opinion.

erally less informed about the trial. In this chapter, it appears that the less informed respondents were the ones most likely to accept the prosecution's case. Together, these findings suggest that the more anti-Semitic tended to accept the prosecution's image of Eichmann, while the less anti-Semitic rejected it. Inded, this paradoxical conclusion is generally supported by the data, although there is also some evidence that those who rejected the prosecution's case entirely—those who saw Eichmann as a guiltless bureaucrat—were influenced by unfriendly attitudes toward Jews.

Table 22 shows the percentage of the people holding each

TABLE 22. ANTI-SEMITISM AND IMAGES OF EICHMANN'S COMPLICITY AND GUILT
(white respondents only)

Per Cent Who Scored Anti-Semitic on:	*Images of Eichmann's Complicity and Guilt* Monster (guilty)	Zealot (guilty)	Guilty Bureaucrat	Guiltless Bureaucrat
General index	38%	38%	30%	43%
Number	(47)	(77)	(36)	(7)
Discrimination index	20%	17%	8%	29%
Number	(50)	(82)	(39)	(7)
Self-segregation index	48%	47%	41%	57%
Number	(48)	(75)	(34)	(7)

of the four images who scored as anti-Semitic on the three measures described earlier. It is clear that no matter what measure of anti-Semitism is used, those who saw Eichmann as a guilty bureaucrat are the least anti-Semitic of all groups. On every measure they are less likely to be anti-Semitic than those who hold the zealot or the monster image. They are also less likely to be anti-Semitic than those who saw Eichmann as a guiltless bureaucrat. This last group appears to be the most consistently anti-Semitic of all six image groups.[15]

[15] The imageless were the most anti-Semitic on the general anti-Semitism index. This appears to be a function of their generally low sophistication

One interpretation is that the anti-Semitism of the uninformed or unsophisticated was simply not engaged by the Eichmann trial. They were apparently too unsophisticated or too uninterested to perceive a connection between the Eichmann trial and their own feelings of ambivalence or hostility toward Jews.[16] There was, however, a small group of sophisticated respondents who, precisely because they were sophisticated, were able to see a connection between the trial and their anti-Semitism, and they judged Eichmann to be not guilty.

In sum, the monster and zealot images attracted the unknowledgeable respondents irrespective of their anti-Semitism. In much the same way, the guilty bureaucrat image of Eichmann attracted knowledgeable respondents, especially

---

level. The evidence supports the view that genuine ignorance of the facts rather than anti-Semitism led to the absence of opinions on the part of the imageless. On two of the three anti-Semitism measures, the imageless who said Eichmann was guilty were more anti-Semitic than those who had no opinion.

[16] This interpretation cannot be satisfactorily tested with the data since the number of cases do not allow comparing the anti-Semitism of the different image groups holding privilege and knowledge constant simultaneously. The table below, using the general anti-Semitism index, shows the results when knowledge alone is held constant (number of cases is shown in parentheses). Insofar as any inference is warranted by the few cases, the findings support the conclusion that, except for those who believed Eichmann not guilty, anti-Semitism did not determine the image of Eichmann among the knowledgeable. Among the unknowledgeable, anti-Semitism was related to image, but in an inverse way: The greater the acceptance of the prosecution's case, the more anti-Semitism was present. This inverse relation appears to be a function of the fact that the most sophisticated were the least disposed to be anti-Semitic and the most disposed to take a sophisticated view of Eichmann's role.

	High Knowledge		*Low Knowledge*	
Image	Per cent Anti-Semitic	Total Number	Per cent Anti-Semitic	Total Number
Monster	28%	(18)	45%	(29)
Zealot	30	(30)	42	(47)
Guilty bureaucrat	30	(23)	31	(13)
Guiltless bureaucrat	50	(6)		(1)

when they were also sophisticated, irrespective of their anti-Semitism. The somewhat lower proportion of anti-Semites among those who held Eichmann to be a guilty subordinate can be accounted for by the fact that the sophisticated tended on the whole to be less anti-Semitic than the unsophisticated. Nevertheless, anti-Semitism played a role, though its influence seems to have been confined to a small group who were both knowledgeable and sophisticated.

NEGRO RESPONSE TO EICHMANN'S ROLE

The Negroes of Oakland, as was seen earlier, gave considerably less attention to the trial than the whites. This was in part a function of their relatively greater disprivilege, but even at the same privilege level, Negroes were always less likely to be informed about the trial than whites. Despite this difference, the first impression conveyed by the data is that Negroes and whites responded to the questions about Eichmann's complicity and guilt in roughly equivalent ways. Of the whites, 55 per cent who were aware of the trial saw Eichmann in terms of one of the images that the prosecution had intended, namely as a monster or zealot. The comparable figure for Negroes was 50 per cent. As in the white community, an image of Eichmann as monster or zealot more often produced a verdict of guilty than an image of him as a bureaucrat. And, again as in the white community, those Negroes without an image of Eichmann's complicity were also least likely to have an opinion on his guilt.

This initial impression of similarity is quickly dissipated when the data are probed more deeply. Dissimilarities first begin to appear with reference to the propensity of the two groups to see Eichmann as guilty. Among those individuals aware of the trial, the Negroes were less likely, whatever their image of Eichmann's complicity, to see him as guilty; 62 per cent of the Negroes judged Eichmann to be guilty as compared with 77 per cent of the whites. This is in part a result of the Negroes' being less likely to have an opinion on Eichmann's guilt; 26 per cent of the Negroes said they had no opinion as compared to 19 per cent of the whites. Negroes, however, were also less likely to judge Eichmann as guilty even when they did have an opinion: 84 per cent of the Negroes with an opinion judged Eichmann guilty as compared with 95 per cent of the whites with an opinion. These differences cannot be explained by differences in knowledge and sophistication in the two groups. At each level of knowledge and sophistication, Negroes were less disposed than whites to see Eichmann as guilty.

A more startling difference between white and Negro responses emerges when analysis turns to the sources of the different images of Eichmann's complicity and guilt. In the white community, it will be recalled, the more sophisticated and knowledgeable a person was, the less likely he was to accept unequivocally the prosecution's case against Eichmann. In the Negro community, an opposite result was obtained. Acceptance of the prosecution's case came largely from the more knowledgeable, rejection largely from the unknowledgeable.

This countertendency in the Negro community was first seen by comparing the knowledgeability of those holding to different images (Table 23). However knowledgeability was defined, Negro respondents with the monster image turned out to be the most knowledgeable, those with the zealot image slightly less knowledgeable, and those with the bureaucrat image the least knowledgeable. In fact, using the same criterion of knowledgeability that was used for whites, none of those who held the bureaucrat image scored as knowledgeable.

The small number of Negroes in the sample, together with

the fact that almost all scored relatively low on the privilege index, makes it impossible to analyze the role of sophistica-

TABLE 23. KNOWLEDGEABILITY AND IMAGES OF EICHMANN'S COMPLICITY AND GUILT
(Negro respondents only)

	Knowledgeability			
	3–4 Items Answered Correctly		2–4 Items Answered Correctly	
Image	Per Cent	Number	Per Cent	Number
Monster (guilty)	18%	(17)	53%	(17)
Zealot (guilty)	13	(30)	20	(30)
Guilty bureaucrat	0	(13)	8	(13)
Guiltless bureaucrat	0	(12)	8	(12)

tion with any degree of confidence. So far as it is possible to determine, however, sophistication or privilege did not modify the fundamental influence of knowledge. Even when he was relatively sophisticated, the informed Negro continued to overselect the monster and zealot images and to underselect the bureaucrat image. Similarly, even when he was unsophisticated, the uninformed Negro continued to overselect the bureaucrat image and to underselect the others.[17]

The data themselves provide no explanation for this countertendency among Negroes. Only speculation concerning the results is possible. The crucial factor may be that the sophisticated and informed Negro, while *objectively* similar to the sophisticated and informed white, is *subjectively* closer to the unsophisticated and uninformed white. Similarly, Negroes who score as unsophisticated and uninformed are more so *subjectively* than the unsophisticated and uninformed whites whom they *objectively* appear to resemble. In other

[17] Of 6 Negroes who scored as knowledgeable (answered three or four knowledge items correctly) and as sophisticated (scored 3 or 4 on the privilege index), 2 chose the monster image, 2 the zealot image, and 2 were imageless; none chose the bureaucrat image. Of 36 Negroes who were unsophisticated and unknowledgeable, 9 chose the monster image, 19 the zealot image, and 10 the bureaucrat image.

words, given the society's general propensity to assign second-class citizenship to the Negro, he is inexorably given less access to the larger society than whites, whatever his achievements. If this is so, the response of Negroes to Eichmann's role may be less a function of their degree of sophistication and knowledge than of the extent to which they are alienated from the white society.

The very fact that the knowledgeable Negro became knowledgeable suggests a certain lack of alienation from the white community, its institutions, and its opinions. However, because of the precariousness of his position in the larger society, the knowledgeable Negro may be led to a certain overconformity. He may not feel free to engage in the kind of cognitive criticism of the trial that the knowledgeable white respondents felt free to exercise. Perhaps for this reason the knowledgeable Negro behaved more like the uninformed white than like the informed white. Like the uninformed white, he accepted uncritically the image of Eichmann projected by the mass media, and did so even when he was relatively sophisticated.

Negroes of low privilege with little knowledge of the trial are likely to be those most alienated from white society. They are rejected by it and, as a consequence, are probably inclined to respond in kind. In rejecting the mass media image of Eichmann, therefore, these Negroes may be expressing hostility, not to the trial itself, but to white institutions and the opinions of the white mass media. There is no evidence for this in the data beyond the fact that the unknowledgeable Negro, unlike the unknowledgeable white, tended to reject the mass media image of Eichmann and to do so even when he was unsophisticated. Unknowledgeable Negroes knew very little about the trial; on the average they knew less than the unknowledgeable whites. But the latter accepted what they discerned as the mass media image of Eichmann while the former rejected what little they saw. Of the eight scapegoat images, three were held by unknowledgeable Negroes, and all three judged Eichmann not guilty.

Apparently this rejection was not motivated by anti-Semitism. While the less privileged, uninformed Negroes were more disposed to be anti-Semitic than their more privileged and informed counterparts, the anti-Semites among them showed no consistent tendency to be more critical of the trial than those who scored as nonanti-Semitic on the measure used.

Summary and Conclusions

From the prosecution's point of view, the case against Eichmann was relatively unambiguous. The evidence of Eichmann's active complicity in the Nazi atrocities against Jews was eminently clear and provided more than ample grounds to support a verdict of guilty. This absence of ambiguity was not entirely reflected, however, in the way that the mass media reported and interpreted the trial. In part, this was because the mass media had a responsibility to report the case for the defense. It arose also because more sophisticated observers of the trial, sensitive to the trial's broader educational goals, raised questions about the strategy of the prosecution's case.

The majority of the public, apparently unaware of the ambiguities, identified with the prosecution's depiction of Eichmann's complicity and guilt. There was a substantial minority who, while convinced of Eichmann's guilt, refused to see Eichmann as more than a responsible bureaucrat, a view of Eichmann's complicity that the prosecution itself had rejected. Only a handful of people were led to a verdict of not guilty.

White respondents who identified wholly with the prosecution's case tended to be characterized by lack of sophistication and information about the trial. In turn, those who were less accepting of the prosecution's claims were on the average the more informed and the more sophisticated. By and large, attitudes about Eichmann's complicity and guilt were not found to be related to feelings of anti-Semitism. In fact, except among a very few knowledgeable people of high sophistication who saw Eichmann as a guiltless bureaucrat, feelings of anti-Semitism were apparently not engaged by this aspect of the trial.

The Negro community of Oakland was less likely than the white community to consider Eichmann guilty though it shared white views of the nature of his complicity. However, Negroes who saw Eichmann as a monster or zealot were more likely to be sophisticated and informed than those who saw him as a bureaucrat. In this respect, Negroes differed sharply from whites, a difference which was interpreted as resulting from the Negro's drastically different status in society. As among whites, feelings of anti-Semitism were apparently not an important element in influencing Negro images of Eichmann's complicity and guilt.

The significance of these results cannot be understood entirely until it is known how a person's assessment of Eichmann's role influenced his recognition of and identification with the trial's educational goals, a matter to be considered in a later chapter. By themselves, the results suggest that the prosecution was reasonably successful in winning the public to its views of Eichmann's role. Certainly a majority agreed in whole or in part with the prosecution's case, and most agreed that Eichmann was guilty. Moreover, even among those who saw Eichmann as nothing more than a bureaucrat, the great majority judged him as guilty.

Despite these outward signs of success, nagging questions remain. About a third of the public did not pay enough attention to the trial either to know that it was going on or to have an opinion about Eichmann's guilt. And, among those who did have an opinion, there is the disturbing note that it was the less discerning part of the public that was most disposed to go along with the prosecution's case. So far as the analysis permits a judgment, these people were merely giving automatic assent to what they vaguely learned about the trial from the popular mass media. There is no evidence that their judgments were considered ones or that these people were caught up emotionally in the drama of the trial. The fact that many of them saw no contradiction between expressing anti-Semitic feelings and identifying with the prosecution's case suggests an absence of depth in their opinions.

One cannot help but wonder what opinions these people would have formed had the mass media presented the prosecution's case in a less sympathetic light. Uninvolved as they were in the trial, it is conceivable that these people would just as easily have adopted a negative view had the mass media stimulated them to do so. Did the fact that the majority were disposed to identify with the prosecution's case make any difference to their understandings of the more abiding lesson that the trial sought to teach? This question will be examined later in the analysis.

It is also difficult at this juncture to interpret the significance of the more critical attitude the more sophisticated and informed white respondents tended to adopt. It seems unfortunate that the people who had the most solid grounds for forming an opinion chose to be critical. It is also disturbing, despite the small number of cases, that there was a group of knowledgeable and privileged anti-Semites who were sharply critical of the prosecution's case. There is a suggestion here of the familiar pattern that prejudiced people are inclined to interpret events to reinforce their own prejudices. That this did not happen among the unsophisticated and uninformed seems to belie the interpretation. However, this effect can occur only where the stimulus is received with sufficient force so that prejudiced feelings are engaged. In the present case, the stimulus had this effect for a few sophisticated anti-Semites who paid attention; it did not apparently have this effect among those who were unsophisticated or uninformed about the trial.

As for the Negroes, their response to Eichmann's role remains somewhat enigmatic and difficult to evaluate. More informed opinion among Negroes was relatively uncritical. That the uninformed were critical may be largely a fortuitous result if, as was suspected, it reflected a general alienation from white society and not a special hostility toward the trial.

In retrospect, it may have been an error of judgment to sample the Negroes in a number proportionate to their distribution in the population. Had it been realized in advance that their response to the trial was so different from that of the whites, some effort to over-represent them in the sample would have been called for in order to guarantee enough cases for detailed analysis. Nevertheless, it seems worthwhile to report what has been learned about their differential response, if only to encourage more concentrated attention in the future on the distinctive qualities of opinion formation and attitudes in the Negro community.

CHAPTER 4

THE LEGALITY OF THE TRIAL

THE complexity of the legal questions raised by an event like the Eichmann trial would seem to bar most of the public from having opinions on them. However, just as being uninformed was not a major barrier to having an opinion on the defendant's complicity and guilt, so lack of knowledge about the details of the trial and the events leading up to it did not inhibit most people—82 per cent of the awares in the sample—from forming opinions about the trial's legality.

Before analyzing this aspect of public-opinion formation it is necessary to review briefly the three principal questions raised about the trial's legality by commentators in various media as well as by the defense. These bore on the way Eichmann was captured, on Israel's right to try him, and on the ability of an Israeli court to render a fair verdict. Unlike the criticism of the prosecution's case, which was shown in the previous chapter to be largely confined to the more sophisticated journals and did not enter the awareness of the majority of the public, the legal propriety of some of Israel's actions in connection with the trial was widely discussed in the mass media. As a rule the popular press answered the legal questions it raised in such a way as to dispose public opinion in Israel's favor, but this of course publicized the legal issues surrounding the trial.

Eichmann's capture by Israeli agents in Argentina and his

delivery to Israel in an El Al plane troubled many people who discussed the trial. Commentators in media ranging from highbrow magazines to the local press expressed reservations and even condemnations of Israel's procedure, claiming that it was contrary to international law. Sometimes uneasiness regarding the capture took the form of a concern that the so-called kidnaping might redound to the disadvantage of Israel and world Jewry.

In general, sophisticated critics of the capture did not use this issue to impugn Israel's right to try Eichmann or to question the legality of the trial itself. Commentators familiar with international law pointed to precedents indicating that the legality of a trial is not conditioned by the manner in which the defendant is apprehended. Nevertheless, Israel's right to jurisdiction was questioned on other grounds. One argument was that Israel was not a state during World War II when Eichmann helped to perpetrate the atrocities of the Nazi regime. According to some commentators, Israel's laws must be considered ex post facto and therefore inapplicable to Eichmann. Defenders of the trial cited the precedent of the Nuremberg tribunal along with a legal principle articulated at Nuremberg that crimes such as those perpetrated by the Nazis have universally and historically been held to be wrong and that no prior notification of illegality was required. It was argued that, according to the moral and legal code of the entire Western world including that of pre-Nazi Germany, the genocidal policy of the Nazis was inherently and intrinsically extralegal and could not be regarded as legal simply because it was carried on by a government.

The applicability of Israeli laws to a citizen of Germany was also questioned. In international law generally, the laws of a nation are not applicable outside its own boundaries. There are exceptions to the rule: Piracy and traffic in slaves, ships, or women are punishable by whatever state apprehends the offenders. According to some observers, Eichmann's crime fell into the same category. Others, unconvinced, argued that the political crime of genocide is fundamentally different from crimes committed by private individuals, thus raising a new question of international law: Shall there be a body of international law and legal institutions with jurisdiction over nations and national officials? One student of constitutional law, Yosal Rogat, criticized Israel's apprehension of Eichmann on the grounds that, besides being ambiguous under present international law, it did not serve to advance international law to a higher level.[1]

Israeli lawyers under Attorney General Gideon Hausner cited precedents for Israel's actions, just as defense attorney Robert Servatius cited contrary ones. This debate was paralleled by Israel's critics and defenders in the media. Besides replying to critics on every legal point, Israel argued its case on the principle of a "higher morality." Premier David Ben-Gurion stated it as follows: "Those whose brothers and sisters were murdered by Eichmann and who undertook to search him out were right morally although perhaps not formally. I know they committed a breach of law, but sometimes there are moral obligations higher than formal law." Ben-Gurion also argued that "it is historic justice that [Eichmann] be tried by a Jewish state. Only a Jewish state can try him, from a moral point of view."[2]

The trial itself did not and could not settle the legal issues it raised. These are likely to remain a continuing source of debate and controversy. But the raising of legal issues introduced an additional factor into public response. Not only did 82 per cent of those who knew about the trial have an opinion,

[1] *The Eichmann Trial and the Rule of Law* (Santa Barbara, Calif.: Center for the Study of Democratic Institutions, Fund for the Republic, November 1961), p. 32.

[2] *New York Times Magazine,* December 18, 1960.

but a substantial minority—27 per cent—had thought enough about the legal issues involved to qualify their responses voluntarily when asked, "Do you think it was legal for Israel to bring Eichmann to trial?" (Table 24).

TABLE 24. VIEWS OF THE TRIAL'S LEGALITY

Reply to: "Do You Think It Was Legal for Israel to Bring Eichmann to Trial?"	Total Awares	Those with Opinions
Definitely yes	41%	50%
Qualified yes	18	22
Qualified no	9	11
Definitely no	14	17
Don't know	18	
Number	(384)	(317)

Of those with an opinion, 50 per cent believed without qualification that the trial was legal. An additional 22 per cent said that they thought it was legal but qualified their answers in some way. The remaining 28 per cent thought that the trial was illegal, 11 per cent adopting this position with qualifications. Altogether, nearly three-quarters of the respondents with an opinion thought that the trial was legal.

The grounds for giving a qualified answer tended to be the same whether the person believed the trial to be legal or illegal. Almost all of the qualifiers—8 out of every 10—mentioned Eichmann's capture in Argentina by Israeli agents as the source of their equivocation. Some, while critical of Israel in this respect, adopted the view of many observers that the capture did not impugn the trial itself.

Yes, legal. They kidnaped him—but I would have done the same thing. It's legal, no matter what method they used.

It may not have been legal to go to another country and arrest him, but from a subjective point of view anyone should be brought to trial for his crimes.

Actually they kidnaped him, which was illegal, but they certainly were justified in bringing him to trial. He certainly needs to be punished.

For others, however, the so-called kidnaping was enough to lead them to judge the entire proceedings as illegal.

No, I don't think they had any right going into another country and kidnaping him. [There are] channels [you] should go through to extradite him.

I don't think it was legal the way that they did it, by kidnaping him. They should have served papers and done it legally.

No, I don't. They had no right to arrest a man in another country and kidnap him out. According to international law, they didn't have the right. Definitely, it's illegal.

The only other qualification raised with any frequency bore on the question of Israel's right to jurisdiction in light of its not being in existence during World War II when the crimes were committed. Again some people were willing to overlook their reservations on the grounds that a "higher justice" was being served, but others were not.

Yes, it was [legal]. Even though Israel was formed after the crimes were committed, many people or relatives in Israel suffered the crimes. So [I] feel it's legal for them to try Eichmann.

From a technical point of view, it wasn't, since the crimes were committed before there was an Israel and the crimes were not committed on Israeli soil.

No, since Israel wasn't a state at the time of the crime.

Only one respondent raised any question about Israel's ability to conduct a fair trial. All in all, the so-called kidnaping was conceived to be the main point at issue. This event was highly publicized at the time it occurred, and of all Israel's actions the most frankly and freely criticized in the mass media. Outright rejection of Israel's jurisdiction did not appear in the mass media, and rarely occurs in the Oakland sample as a spontaneous response.

That few respondents explicitly rejected Israel's right to try Eichmann is one thing; whether people thought it desirable that Israel should try him is another. After the question on legality had been asked, respondents were presented with four possible actions which Israel might have taken with regard to Eichmann, and asked to choose the one which, in their opinion, would have been the right course for the Israeli government to follow. The four possibilities were: try him as they were doing before an Israeli court; hand him over to Germany for trial; hand him over to an international court for trial; let him go free.[3] The idea of trying Eichmann in an international court might not have occurred to many people had the question not brought it to their attention. Nevertheless, 51 per cent of those who knew about the trial would have preferred having it conducted by an international court. Thirty-six per cent favored the *status quo,* i.e., having Israel try Eichmann. There was little sympathy for having Eichmann tried by Germany (4 per cent) and even less for letting him go free (3 per cent). Very few respondents (6 per cent) had no opinion on the question.[4]

Legality as Perceived by the White Community

Most people had an opinion about the trial's legality. Some of them undoubtedly formed their opinions knowing what the

[3] It is recognized that the choice "hand him over to an international court" was not realistic since no such court exists. Nevertheless, it was thought germane to test public opinion on the issue.

[4] As might be expected, there was a strong relationship between responses to this question and the question on legality. Almost all (92 per cent) who preferred having Israel try Eichmann thought that the trial was legal. Among those favoring another course of action, 61 per cent thought the trial was legal.

legal controversy was about. Others found it possible to make a judgment without such knowledge, perhaps even without knowing that legal issues had been raised at all. For them, considerations other than legal ones necessarily influenced their opinions. Moreover, while it is conceivable that an informed person might formulate an opinion on a careful weighing of the legal arguments alone, it seems probable that other considerations influenced him as well. The task of analysis is to identify these other considerations. Level of sophistication, opinions on other aspects of the trial, and feelings of prejudice are three factors to be explored. Basic differences in white and Negro responses once again require that they be considered separately.

In analyzing opinions on Eichmann's complicity and guilt, it was found that when whites had opinions, lack of knowledge concerning the trial produced agreement with the prosecution's case. On the basis of that evidence, one might predict with some confidence that the uninformed respondents would also tend to accept the legality of the trial. They would be unlikely to have heard of the so-called kidnaping or to have read the criticisms that appeared in the mass media. They would be even less likely to have heard of the other legal questions raised in connection with the trial, especially in the more sophisticated journals. In effect, they would have no reason to doubt the legality of the trial.

But what about the knowledgeable? Many of them knew the facts of the capture of Eichmann, either in whole or in part. On the ground that knowledge of the capture was one possible avenue for rejecting the legality of the trial, one might predict that the informed would exhibit doubts more frequently than the uninformed. Further, the knowledgeable were more likely to be acquainted with the other legal issues discussed in the sophisticated media. Quite apart from the kidnaping, therefore, the knowledgeable might be expected to have grounds for questioning the legality of the trial that were outside the purview of the unknowledgeable.

On the other hand, the knowledgeable were also more likely to know who Eichmann was and to have a correct picture of the extent of the Nazi atrocities. Such knowledge could presumably evoke sympathy for Israel's cause and lead to a perception of the trial as legal. Although they were informed about the details of Eichmann's capture and other legal issues, the knowledgeable might nevertheless decide that the trial itself was legal.

In order to find out how knowledge concerning Eichmann's arrest influenced opinions on legality, respondents were divided into four groups: those who knew that Israel had captured Eichmann in Argentina; those who knew only that Israel had captured him; those who knew only the place of his capture; and those who were uninformed as to either fact. For each group, it was then determined what proportion thought of the trial as legal.

Table 25, which presents the results of this analysis, suggests that knowledge of the kidnaping was an important factor in leading respondents to view the trial as illegal.

TABLE 25. VIEWS OF THE TRIAL'S LEGALITY BY KNOWLEDGE OF EICHMANN'S CAPTURE
(white respondents only)

Views on Trial's Legality	*Respondents' Knowledge of Eichmann's Capture* Knew Both Israel and Argentina	Knew Argentina Only	Knew Israel Only	Uninformed on Both Questions
Legal	46%	71%	70%	88%
Illegal	54	29	30	12
Number with an opinion	(84)	(14)	(61)	(72)
Don't know	8%	0%	18%	26%
Total number	(91)	(14)	(74)	(97)

Among those who knew both where and by whom Eichmann had been arrested, less than half (46 per cent) judged the trial to be legal. Among those who were completely uninformed on the capture, an overwhelming majority (88 per cent) saw the trial as legal. Those with partial knowledge fall between the two extremes; whether respondents knew only that Argentina was the country in which Eichmann was capture or only that Israel captured him, about 70 per cent thought that the trial was legal.

Table 25 also shows that the completely unknowledgeable group had the highest proportion of "don't know" responses on legality. Possessing information about Eichmann's capture was conducive, then, to having an opinion *and* to having a negative opinion on the trial's legality.

It was speculated above that knowing who Eichmann was and the extent of the Nazi atrocities might counteract the tendency of the capture to make for a judgment of illegality. In order to test this proposition, the sample was again divided into four groups: those who knew that Eichmann was a Nazi and that 6 million Jews had been killed; those who knew only that Eichmann was a Nazi; those who knew only that 6 million Jews had been killed; and those who were ignorant on both items. The way in which each of these four groups responded to the question on legality was then tabulated. As Table 26 shows, the relation is similar to the one, just presented, between knowledge on the capture and legality. That is to say, knowledge of the facts about Eichmann and the Nazi atrocities did *not* induce people to see the trial as legal. On the contrary, those who knew both facts showed the least disposition to see the trial as legal, while those who were uninformed on both questions were the most disposed to see the trial as legal.

Further inspection of Table 26 reveals that knowledge of Eichmann's identity had virtually no influence on judgments of the legality of the trial. The major difference is between those who knew the official estimate of 6 million Jews killed and those who did not, with the former much more disposed than the latter to see the trial as illegal.

TABLE 26. VIEWS OF THE TRIAL'S LEGALITY BY KNOWLEDGE OF NAZI ATROCITIES
(white respondents only)

	Knowledge of Eichmann's Identity and Nazi Atrocities			
Views on Trial's Legality	Knew Both Nazi and 6,000,000	Knew 6,000,000 Only	Knew Nazi Only	Uninformed on Both
Legal	55%	58%	74%	75%
Illegal	45	42	26	25
Number with an opinion	(69)	(19)	(92)	(51)
Don't know	9%	21%	12%	28%
Total number	(76)	(24)	(105)	(71)

The results on legality parallel the earlier results on respondents' images of Eichmann. Being informed on the trial was associated with a tendency to reject the prosecution's case. It did not matter whether respondents were informed on the capture or on the Nazi atrocities; in either case, as Tables 25 and 26 showed, knowledge was correlated with judging the trial to be illegal.

But the two kinds of knowledge did not play equally important roles. This can be seen in Table 27, which compares the relative influence of both kinds of knowledge on judgments that the trial was legal. That knowledge of the atrocities did *not* dispose people to regard the trial as legal is again evident from an inspection of the rows in Table 27. Regardless of how much they knew about the capture, respondents who knew the official estimate of 6 million Jews killed were consistently *less* likely to say that the trial was legal than those who did not have correct information on this score. The differences are small, however; in one case, the difference is 10 percentage points, in the other 5. Looking now at the columns of Table 27, it can be seen that knowledge of the capture had a considerable effect on judgments of the trial's

TABLE 27. VIEWS OF THE TRIAL'S LEGALITY BY KNOWLEDGE OF EICHMANN'S CAPTURE AND NAZI ATROCITIES
(white respondents only)

	Knowledge of the Nazi Atrocities		
Per Cent Judging Trial as Legal Among Those with:	Knew 6 Million	Did Not Know 6 Million	Difference in Percentage Points
Complete knowledge of capture[a]	42%	52%	10
Number	(52)	(32)	
Incomplete knowledge of capture[a]	75%	80%	5
Number	(36)	(111)	
Difference in percentage points	33	28	

[a] Complete knowledge of capture includes those who knew both that Eichmann had been captured in Argentina and that Israel was the capturing country; all others are combined under incomplete knowledge.

NOTE: The proportion responding "don't know" in each of the four cells of the table is as follows:

	Knew 6 Million		*Did Not Know 6 Million*	
Complete knowledge	0%	(58)	3%	(33)
Incomplete knowledge	14	(42)	22	(143)

legality. Regardless of their knowledge of the Nazi atrocities, respondents who were well informed on the capture were much less likely to characterize the trial as legal than their less knowledgeable counterparts. In one case, the percentage point difference is 33, in the other 28. Thus, while knowledge of the atrocities was associated with rejection of the legality of the trial, the relation is slight. This cannot be said of knowledge of the capture. When people knew the details of the so-called kidnaping, they tended to believe the trial was illegal.

Table 27 reflects the general tendency, already observed, for knowledge to be associated with a more skeptical view of the trial. On the question of legality, knowledge of Eichmann's abduction had a particularly decisive influence. Once again, rejection of the prosecution's position was most frequent among the well informed, acceptance most frequent among the poorly informed.

In analyzing images of Eichmann, it was found that among the knowledgeable, sophistication (as measured by social privilege) tended to reinforce skepticism about the prosecution's case. What was its influence on public perceptions of the trial's legality? The answer is to be found in Table 28.

TABLE 28. VIEWS OF THE TRIAL'S LEGALITY BY LEVEL OF SOPHISTICATION AND KNOWLEDGE OF CAPTURE
(white respondents only)

Per Cent Judging Trial as Legal Among Those with:	*Level of Sophistication* Low	Medium	High
Complete knowledge of capture	77%	55%	30%
Number	(13)	(31)	(40)
Incomplete knowledge of capture	87%	84%	63%
Number	(38)	(64)	(43)

NOTE: The proportion responding "don't know" in each of the six cells of the table is as follows:

	Low		*Medium*		*High*	
Complete knowledge	0%	(13)	6%	(33)	11%	(45)
Incomplete knowledge	30	(54)	18	(78)	14	(50)

Sophistication once again leads to increased skepticism, and its impact is greatest where the respondent is well informed on the capture. Among those who had complete knowledge, the proportion who regarded the trial as legal decreases sharply—from 77 per cent to 55 per cent to a minority of 30 per cent—as level of sophistication rises. Among those not completely informed of the capture, persons with medium sophistication were as likely to see the trial as legal (84 per cent) as those with low sophistication (87 per cent). However, among the highly sophisticated who were uninformed, there was a noticeable decline in the proportion saying that the trial was legal (63 per cent).

Table 28 also continues to confirm the basic finding that knowledge of Eichmann's capture was a critical factor in inducing people to regard the trial as illegal. At every sophistication level, knowledgeable respondents were less disposed to see the trial as legal than their unknowledgeable counterparts. As in the case of respondents' images of Eichmann's complicity and guilt, knowledge and sophistication combined to produce high levels of rejection of the prosecution's case.

In the preceding chapter, it was suggested that the agreement of the unknowledgeable and unsophisticated with the prosecution's case was more apparent than real, that these people were merely expressing their dim perception of the image of Eichmann projected by the mass media. Without being aware of the evidence introduced at the trial, they concluded that, since Eichmann was being tried and characterized as a murderer, he must certainly have personally murdered. Of the three images of Eichmann—monster, zealot, and guilty bureaucrat—that of monster was the least ambiguous. It represented the most conventional interpretation of his crimes and legal responsibility and provided the most nearly unequivocal grounds for judging him guilty. The zealot image was also highly chosen by the unknowledgeable but by the more sophisticated among them, and could not be characterized as necessarily stemming from an oversimplistic interpretation of Eichmann's crimes. Those who saw Eichmann as a bureaucrat but as nevertheless guilty tended to be the sophisticated and knowledgeable; these people were capable of entertaining a nonconventional, ambiguous, and complex notion of legal responsibility. Finally, those who saw

Eichmann as a bureaucrat but as innocent were, of course, not characterized in these terms, but were seen as being on a different dimension. So far as could be determined, there was a tendency for the responses of this group to be motivated by anti-Semitic feelings rather than by their high knowledge and sophistication.

Acceptance of the trial as legal can also be characterized as the conventional, easy, and unambiguous position. To the extent that this is so, a respondent's image of Eichmann will presumably be related to his views of the legality of the trial. Examination of Table 29 reveals that such a relation does

TABLE 29. VIEWS OF THE TRIAL'S LEGALITY BY IMAGES OF EICHMANN (white respondents only)

	Image of Eichmann's Role[a]			
Views on Legality	Monster	Zealot	Guilty Bureaucrat	Guiltless Bureaucrat
Legal	85%	67%	61%	29%
Illegal	15	33	39	71
Number with an opinion	(48)	(75)	(31)	(7)
Don't know	4%	8%	21%	0%
Total number	(50)	(82)	(39)	(7)

[a] As might be predicted, the imageless were the least likely to have an opinion on legality. Twenty-four per cent of the 33 imageless-guilty said they had no opinion on legality. Of the 17 people who were imageless-no opinion, 47 per cent said they had no opinion on the trial's legality. Among those with an opinion, 72 per cent of the imageless-guilty saw the trial as legal as compared to 44 per cent of the imageless-no opinion.

exist. Of those who held the monster image, 85 per cent said that the trial was legal. Among those who held the zealot and the guilty bureaucrat images the percentage who saw the trial as legal drops to 67 per cent and 61 per cent respectively. The figure for those who held the zealot image is much closer to the 61 per cent for the guilty bureaucrat image than it is to the 86 per cent for the monster image. In an indirect way this confirms the impression noted in the last chapter that, while for many people the zealot image was a conformist one, for many others it was not, but represented a rational evaluation of the prosecution's case. As might be predicted, the percentage of legal verdicts among those who saw Eichmann as an innocent bureaucrat is very low; the figure is 29 per cent.[5]

Table 29 supports the prediction that images and views on legality would be consistently and systematically related. The monster image was apparently chosen by some because it was a conventional and unambiguous image of Eichmann, but presumably those people who chose the monster image on the basis of knowledge of the details of the Eichmann trial did so objectively and not because it presented an easy way of coming to the conclusion that Eichmann was guilty. If this is so, it would be expected that people who formed the monster image on the basis of knowledge of the trial would be no more conventionally oriented than people who chose the zealot or the guilty bureaucrat image. Among the knowledgeable, no differences ought to be found in their judgments of legality. Table 30 substantiates this expectation. Those who were knowledgeable about the capture show virtually no difference in the percentage who said that the trial was legal. Irrespective of their image, a little over half judged the trial as legal.

On the other hand, judgments that the trial was legal ought still to be most frequent among those who formed the

[5] In interpreting a no-opinion response on legality as reflecting a perception of the ambiguities inherent in the legality question, it is instructive that those who held the monster image were the least likely to have no opinion on the trial's legality (4 per cent). Those who held the zealot image were somewhat more likely to voice no opinion (8 per cent), while those holding the guilty bureaucrat image were the most likely to do so (21 per cent). There were no "don't know" responses among those holding Eichmann to be an innocent bureaucrat. While the number of cases is small, this too is revealing in suggesting that those with this image saw the legality issue in unambiguous, if negative, terms.

monster image without knowledge and less frequent among those who chose the zealot and guilty bureaucrat images without knowledge. Fully 97 per cent of the uninformed holding the monster image said that the trial was legal; sub-

TABLE 30. VIEWS OF THE TRIAL'S LEGALITY BY IMAGES OF EICHMANN AND KNOWLEDGE OF CAPTURE[a]
(white respondents only)

Per Cent Judging Trial as Legal Among Those with:	*Image of Eichmann's Role*[b] Monster	Zealot	Guilty Bureaucrat
Complete knowledge of capture	54%	52%	53%
Number	(13)	(23)	(17)
Incomplete knowledge of capture	97%	73%	71%
Number	(35)	(52)	(14)

[a] Since six out of the seven respondents who saw Eichmann as an innocent bureaucrat were knowledgeable, these have been omitted from this table. The one unknowledgeable person in this group judged the trial to be legal. Among the knowledgeable, five saw the trial as illegal.

[b] Percentages are based on replies by those with an opinion. Distribution of "don't know" responses in the six cells of the table is as follows:

	Monster		*Zealot*		*Guilty Bureaucrat*	
Complete knowledge	0%	(13)	8%	(25)	10%	(19)
Incomplete knowledge	5	(37)	9	(57)	30	(20)

stantially fewer—73 per cent—of the uninformed holding the zealot image held this view. And, indeed, roughly the same proportion (71 per cent) of the unknowledgeable who saw Eichmann as a guilty bureaucrat accepted the trial as legal.

In sum, the point of departure for forming an opinion on the trial's legality was how much one knew about it. Knowledge itself made people aware of the existence of alternative points of view. Particularly decisive was complete knowledge about the capture. That the knowledgeable were more prone to be critical is, in part, simply a result of their knowing that there was something to be critical about.

Sophistication also strongly influenced the response on

legality; with greater sophistication, the response was more likely to be critical. The meaning of this relation, it is suspected, is that sophistication sensitized the already knowledgeable person to the more subtle legal questions raised by Israel's assuming the right of jurisdiction. Being more effectively exposed to the arguments concerning legality, the informed sophisticate simply had greater opportunity to be critical.

What do these findings imply for the influence which prejudice against Jews may have had on judgments of the trial's legality? On purely objective grounds, prejudice is no more relevant a basis for deciding the legality question than is one's opinions of Eichmann's complicity and guilt.[6] The uninformed, however, were not in a position to consider the trial's legality objectively; it is possible, therefore, that they permitted their prejudices to color their views on legality. This is not to say, of course, that the more sophisticated and knowledgeable person would be wholly able to transcend his prejudices, if he had any, and to decide the issue purely on a rational evaluation of both sides of the argument. Comparatively, however, he was in a position to do this whereas the uninformed person was not.

These expectations received some, though relatively slight, confirmation. Table 31 shows that whether or not a person was sophisticated or knowledgeable, there was slightly less likelihood that he would see the trial as legal if he were prejudiced against Jews than if he were not. Moreover, prejudice had a slightly greater effect among those without complete knowledge than among those with complete knowledge of the capture.

Compared to the powerful influence which knowledge and

[6] From a strictly legal point of view, there is no relation between the guilt or innocence of a defendant and the legality of the procedures by which he is tried. In fact, procedural safeguards have been designed to prevent a trial from being considered legitimate merely on the grounds of a general consensus of the defendant's guilt.

sophistication had on responses—revealed once again in Table 31—the effect of prejudice is negligible.[7] The explanation for this may rest in the mounting evidence that the trial did not engage the public's attention and interest in a distinctive way. Unlike the Freedom Rider issue for the Negroes, people were not persuaded that the trial was an event with important personal implications for them. The fact that the trial did not engage people's prejudices may be viewed as a sign of its failure to establish a connection between the Nazi atrocities and the holding of prejudiced attitudes toward

TABLE 31. VIEWS OF THE TRIAL'S LEGALITY BY SOPHISTICATION, KNOWLEDGE, AND ANTI-SEMITISM
(white respondents only)

	LEVEL OF KNOWLEDGE AND SOPHISTICATION[a]			
PER CENT JUDGING TRIAL AS LEGAL AMONG:[b]	*Knowledgeable* Sophisticated	*Knowledgeable* Unsophisticated	*Unknowledgeable* Sophisticated	*Unknowledgeable* Unsophisticated
Prejudiced[c]	25% (8)	59% (17)	57% (14)	81% (42)
Unprejudiced	29 (31)	65 (23)	71 (24)	90 (51)
Percentage point difference	4	6	14	9

[a] Respondents were divided according to whether or not they had complete knowledge of the capture and according to whether they were highly sophisticated (scored 4 or 5 on the privilege index) or less than highly sophisticated (scored 0 to 3 on the privilege index). The number of respondents in each category is shown in parentheses.

[b] Percentages represent proportions who said trial was legal out of the total with an opinion. The proportion responding "don't know" in each of the eight cells of the table is as follows:

	Sophisticated	*Unsophisticated*	*Sophisticated*	*Unsophisticated*
Prejudiced	11% (9)	0% (17)	0% (14)	26% (57)
Unprejudiced	9 (34)	8 (25)	17 (29)	14 (59)

[c] The prejudiced are those who scored 1 or more on the general anti-Semitism index. The unprejudiced are those who scored zero on this index.

[7] This conclusion is also supported using the other measures of anti-Semitism. Whatever measure is used, anti-Semitism has neither a large nor a consistent relation to views on legality.

Jews. Although further analysis may refine or change this interpretation, it is the only conclusion consistent with the evidence examined thus far.

The Negro Response

Negroes, it will be recalled, were generally less accepting than whites of the prosecution's case against Eichmann, but they were considerably more accepting than whites of the trial's legality (Table 32). Among those with an opinion, 86

Table 32. Views of the Trial's Legality by Race

Views on Trial's Legality	Negroes	Whites
Definitely legal	71%	42%
Qualified legal	15	25
Qualified illegal	4	14
Definitely illegal	10	19
Number with an opinion	(73)	(231)
Don't know	22%	16%
Total number	(93)	(276)

per cent of the Negroes said that the trial was legal, as compared with 67 per cent of the whites. Negroes were also less likely to qualify their responses. Seventy-one per cent of the Negroes, as compared to 42 per cent of the whites, thought that the trial was definitely legal. As might be expected, Negroes were less likely to have an opinion on legality, but not substantially so; 22 per cent of the Negroes and 16 per cent of the whites had no opinion on the trial's legality.

Negroes who had no opinion were disproportionately drawn from persons who did not know any of the facts of the trial, had an incomplete or no image of Eichmann's complicity and guilt, or were relatively the least privileged. Among the group sharing all of these characteristics, 46 per cent said they had no opinion on the legality question (15 out of 33). The comparable figure for the rest of the Negroes was 7 per cent (4 out of 60). Saying "don't know" was clearly not a means adopted to express one's ambivalence or to avoid making one's position known. For the most part, a "don't know" response among the Negroes appears to reflect a genuine absence of opinion.

Concentrating on those with an opinion, a reasonable assumption is that the Negroes' greater acceptance of the trial's legality is simply a consequence of their generally lower level of knowledge about the trial and their relative lack of sophistication compared to whites. Whites who were uninformed and unsophisticated were highly inclined to see the trial as legal. It would appear to follow that the same factors were operating in the Negro community, except with greater force, and would therefore account for the Negro response.

Such an expectation, however, runs counter to what was learned in the previous chapter about Negro reaction to Eichmann's complicity and guilt. There, it will be recalled, knowledge and sophistication contributed to a greater rather than a decreased acceptance of the prosecution's case. Why does this same tendency not carry over to acceptance of the trial's legality?

Trying to understand how the Negro response came about is complicated by the fact that only 73 Negroes had an opinion on the legality question and, among these, only 10 thought that the trial was illegal. Among the 63 who thought the trial was legal, 11 qualified their responses; to provide a somewhat more solid basis for conducting the analysis, these will be combined with the illegal responses.[8] The analytical question to be answered is: What contributed to the Negroes' unqualifiedly legal response?

[8] This method does not change the direction of the results, nor, for that matter, does it provide a sufficient number of cases on which to base entirely firm conclusions. Nevertheless, some tentative observations about the way in which they were patterned are warranted.

Few of the Negroes with an opinion on the trial's legality knew the answers to the two simple, factual questions asked about Eichmann's capture—6 out of the 73 knew both facts, 14 knew one of the two facts, the vast majority knew neither. Among the completely informed, 3 (or 50 per cent) thought that the trial was definitely legal. Ten of the 14 with partial information (72 per cent) and 39 of the 53 uninformed (74 per cent) felt this way. Although the number of cases is small, these findings coincide with those for the white sample, and support the hypothesis advanced earlier that their relatively lower knowledge might help to explain the Negroes' greater acceptance of the trial's legality.

At the same time, this result appears to be discrepant with the earlier finding that knowledgeable Negroes were more likely to identify with the prosecution's depiction of Eichmann's role. What does agree with the earlier results, however, is that among the 67 Negroes who were less than completely informed, greater sophistication is associated with an opinion that the trial was definitely legal (Table 33). Although the number of cases is small, the consistency of the result, that every increase in sophistication is accompanied by an increase in the proportion of unqualified opinions that the trial was legal, lends confidence that the effect is a genuine one.

TABLE 33. VIEWS OF THE TRIAL'S LEGALITY BY SOPHISTICATION (Negro respondents only)

	Level of Sophistication				
	Low 0	1	2	3	High 4
Per cent saying trial was definitely legal	54%	71%	78%	90%	[a]
Number	(13)	(24)	(18)	(10)	(2)

[a] Too few cases to report a percentage.

What these results suggest—and they are no more than

suggestive—is that knowledge of Eichmann's capture had the effect among both Negroes and whites of increasing the chances that a person would conceive of the trial as being other than legal. Among whites, being sophisticated tended to reinforce this propensity. Among Negroes, sophistication had the opposite effect of producing greater identification with Israel's position.

Again it is possible only to surmise an explanation of this. The interpretation that suggests itself is essentially the one advanced to account for the greater propensity of the sophisticated Negro to accept the prosecution's case against Eichmann. As Negroes increase in their level of sophistication (or privilege), they tend to identify with the values they perceive through the mass media to be held by the white community. In turn, the greater hostility exhibited by unsophisticated Negroes reflects their general alienation from white society.

This is as far as the analysis ought to be pursued; as it is, the limits of good research practice have already been pushed to an extreme. However, the temptation to see whether prejudice played any consistent role in informing the Negro responses could not be resisted. The exploration was unrewarding. If prejudice had any effect on the Negro responses, it was more subtle than the measuring instruments were able to detect with so small a sample.

Summary and Conclusions

This chapter has been concerned with examining the public's response to questions raised about the trial's legality. In the absence of an unambiguous body of international law dealing with the crimes of governments, it was inevitable that Israel's right to jurisdiction over Eichmann would be questioned. The ambiguity and complexities of the legal issues were not, however, major deterrents to opinion formation, and most people were able to state a position either pro or con. A substantial majority—72 per cent—of those who had an opinion had a positive one and said that they thought the trial was legal. This view, however, was frequently accompanied by the opinion that it would have been preferable, all things considered, had Eichmann been tried by an international court.

Almost a prerequisite to viewing the trial's legality in other than positive terms was some knowledge of the legal issues raised. With such knowledge, the chances were about even that a person would perceive the trial as illegal. Among the wholly ignorant, the chances were one out of ten. The powerful influence of knowledge on opinion, it was concluded, was largely a consequence of its making the alternatives visible. For the uninformed, there were few, if any, grounds for thinking that the trial might have been illegal.

While it was expected that knowledge of the legal issues might predispose people to question the legality of the trial, it was also thought that this effect would be mitigated by knowledge of the Nazi atrocities. People with such knowledge, it was suspected, would be more inclined to see the trial as legal out of sympathy with Israel's cause. The results did not confirm the expectation. In fact, knowledge of the Nazi atrocities increased, rather than decreased, the likelihood that the trial would be viewed as illegal. However, its importance was relatively slight as compared with knowledge about the capture.

Skepticism was also found to be associated with sophistication; in this chapter, a marked relationship was found between the public's level of sophistication and its rejection of the trial's legality. The effect of sophistication was particularly strong among the informed; among those who were both sophisticated and informed, 2 out of 3 felt that the trial was illegal. In sharp contrast, 3 out of 4 of the least sophisticated accepted the legality of the trial, even when they had complete knowledge of the capture. Knowledge sensitized people to the ambiguities surrounding the trial's legality; when knowledge was combined with sophistication, these ambiguities were resolved in favor of the judgment that the trial was illegal.

People who were uninformed about the capture were not in a position to decide the legality question on objective grounds. For them, it would have been appropriate to acknowledge this and respond "don't know." Few took this path. This raised the question as to how such people did form their opinions. One clue was found in the discovery that, among the uninformed, those who believed that Eichmann had personally killed were almost unanimous in their opinion that the trial was legal. Apparently, having accepted the most unambiguous image of Eichmann's role, they were readily inclined to accept the legality of the trial. It was also suspected that whether or not they were prejudiced against Jews would also influence the responses of the uninformed, unsophisticated respondents. There was a slight tendency in this direction but, by and large, the evidence indicated that for most people, their prejudice against Jews was not significantly engaged by the trial.

Analysis of the Negro response was circumscribed by the small number of cases. Insofar as analysis was possible, the patterning of Negro answers paralleled that in the white community with respect to the influence of both knowledge and prejudice. The few Negroes who were knowledgeable were less accepting of the trial's legality and, as in the white community, prejudice was not a factor in forming Negro attitudes. Contrary to what was found for whites, sophistication had the effect of increasing, rather than decreasing, agreement with Israel's position.

All in all, Israel succeeded in winning the public to her

view on the trial's legality to about the same degree as she succeeded in gaining acceptance of the prosecution's image of Eichmann's complicity and guilt. However, her success was much greater in both instances among the uninformed and unsophisticated majority than it was among the informed and sophisticated elite. It is necessary to withhold judgment as to whether the disaffection of the elite represented hostility or simply skepticism, but whatever the answer turns out to be, Israel's failure to capture their support represents something of a defeat.

Whether winning mass support constitutes a victory depends on one's perspective. On the one hand, it would have been highly disturbing to Israel, and to the informed citizenry of the world, had the mass of people exhibited hostility. At the same time, their attitude undoubtedly borders on apathy. Apathy on the part of masses of people contributed to the circumstances which led to the trial. That apathy also contributes to the trial's acceptance is not entirely reassuring.

This is not the time to consider what Israel might have done to involve the public more deeply in the trial and to win greater identification among the elite for her case. Note may be taken in passing, however, that her decision to depict Eichmann as a dedicated Nazi who was more than an underling was apparently, despite the opposition of friendly critics, a fortunate one. At least, greater support for her views on legality, as well as on guilt, was received from those who identified with her position than from those who adopted the position advocated by friendly critics.

There is, once again, much to be said about what the results imply for a more general understanding of anti-Semitism and of public-opinion formation. As before, such comment will be reserved for the final chapter.

CHAPTER 5

EICHMANN'S PUNISHMENT

THE world press assumed that a verdict of guilty would be rendered in the Eichmann trial long before the verdict was actually reached. Consequently, Eichmann's punishment was a matter of discussion and controversy throughout the trial.

Both before and after the sentencing, the most widely held view was that the death penalty was both the proper and the inevitable punishment for Eichmann. Anything less, it was argued, would denigrate the hideousness of Eichmann's crimes. This support for what was essentially the Israeli position was typically the response of America's daily newspapers and broadcast media. In the more specialized journals, however, the issue of punishment was debated with more vigor, and, in the process, the pro's and con's of the death sentence were weighed.

Some opposed the death penalty for Eichmann on the grounds of a general opposition to capital punishment. Such dissent came from Christian religious publications, which stressed not only the Sixth Commandment, but the New Testament injunction against demanding an eye for an eye and a tooth for a tooth. Implicit in some of the reluctance to impose the death penalty was the view that it might have the symbolic consequence of expiating the guilt of the German people, and indeed of the world, for having permitted the Nazi horrors. In Eichman's death, it was argued, the world would see its own atonement. A related view was sometimes expressed that death would be too mild a sentence for Eichmann, that somehow he ought to be made to suffer for his crimes. Finally, some opposition to the death sentence seemed to stem from the feeling that by forgoing the death penalty Israel would be exemplifying that same "higher morality" to which she appealed for support of the trial.

Public Opinion on the Punishment Issue

The citizens of Oakland, it will be recalled, were interviewed for this study just as the trial proceedings were ending but before a verdict was reached. Consequently, they were in no position when interviewed to react to the actual sentence of death. Having been exposed to the evidence of the trial, respondents were asked, figuratively, to perform as members of a jury. With all of the evidence in, what ought the verdict to be? And, if guilty, what sentence ought the jury to recommend?

The overwhelming verdict of respondents with an opinion was that Eichmann was guilty. Among those who personally found Eichmann guilty there was general agreement that the court would also find him guilty. There was no such agreement, however, about how Eichmann would or ought to be punished.

Respondents who both gave and expected a verdict of guilty were asked two questions about his punishment: What sentence do you think the court will impose? What sentence would you personally give him were the matter up to you? The responses of the white members of the sample are reported in Table 34. Because Negroes viewed the punishment issue in a different way, the Negro response is discussed separately.

Looking first at the "Total" figures in the bottom row of

Table 34, it is seen that a bare majority of 55 per cent said they expected the court to impose the death sentence. Twenty-six per cent expected a sentence of life imprisonment. A handful (3 per cent) expected some other sentence

TABLE 34. EICHMANN'S PUNISHMENT: PREFERENCE AND EXPECTATION[a]
(white respondents only)

Punishment Favored	Punishment Expected: Death	Life Imprisonment	Other	Don't Know	*Total*
Death	28%	6%	b	3%	37%
Life imprisonment	21	16	b	6	43
Other	3	2	3	3.	11
Don't know	3	2	b	4	9
Total	55%	26%	3%	16%	100%
Number					(184)

[a] Percentages for this table are based on the total number of white respondents who both expected the court to find Eichmann guilty and also themselves gave a verdict of guilty. Only 184 of the 276 white awares met this dual criterion.

[b] No cases in this cell.

(such as limited imprisonment), and 16 per cent declined to offer a prediction.

Were the matter up to them (look now at the figures in the "Total" column at the right of Table 34), only 37 per cent of the respondents would have personally imposed the death sentence. Almost half—43 per cent—favored a sentence of life imprisonment. Of the balance, 11 per cent favored a different sentence (two persons favored letting Eichmann go free), and 9 per cent said they did not know what sentence they would impose.

If only those who personally advocated death can be presumed to be supporters of the final verdict and in full sympathy with it, then only 37 per cent of the whites can be said to have been satisfied with the verdict. This 37 per cent is outweighed by the 43 per cent who explicitly said they favored life imprisonment. Clearly, 43 per cent represents a fairly high order of possible dissatisfaction with the outcome of the trial.

Only those who believed that Eichmann both was and would be found guilty were queried on his punishment and are being considered here. Yet despite their belief in Eichmann's guilt, almost half of these respondents favored life imprisonment. Even more interesting is that one-quarter—26 per cent—mistakenly believed that life imprisonment would actually be the sentence imposed. The conclusion that emerges from these gross figures is that the public showed a striking tendency toward leniency both in preference and in expectation.

Depending on their responses to the two questions on punishment, respondents can be classified along two main dimensions. They can be separated into those who took a "hard" attitude toward Eichmann's punishment and advocated death, and those who took a "soft" attitude and advocated life imprisonment. They can be further divided into "realists" and "misperceivers," that is, into those who correctly predicted the court punishment of death and those who misperceived the situation by predicting life imprisonment. Cross-classifying these responses yields four types. There are 51 "hard realists," respondents who both preferred and predicted death. Of the four groups this is the largest (28 per cent). Twenty-one per cent or 38 respondents are "soft realists"; they preferred life imprisonment but nevertheless correctly predicted death. The third largest group (16 per cent or 29 respondents) are "soft misperceivers," who both preferred and predicted life imprisonment. Finally, there is a small group of 11 "hard misperceivers" who personally voted death but predicted life imprisonment.[1]

[1] Only these four groups of respondents are analyzed in this chapter. The omission of those who said "other" or "don't know" in answer to one or both of the punishment questions has been dictated in part by the small number of cases and in part by the need to avoid an overcumbersome typology.

In the following analysis attention is focused on a description of the four types in an effort to arrive at some understanding of what led different groups to their preferences and predictions.[2] Do the four groups differ in the extent of their knowledge about the trial, in their attitudes toward one or another aspect of the proceedings, in their social characteristics? Can a preference for life imprisonment be interpreted as a possible sign of hidden sympathy for Eichmann, or perhaps as representing a failure to understand the nature of his crimes? Or did it stem from a more general repugnance to capital punishment having little to do with respondents' judgments of Eichmann and the trial?

The Hard Realists

The portrait of the hard realists that emerges from the analysis is that they were highly uncritical of all aspects of the trial. About three-quarters (76 per cent) accepted the monster or zealot image of Eichmann. They were also very strongly inclined to view the trial as legal (78 per cent); and, more than any other group, they supported Israel's claim of jurisdiction over the alternative of having the trial conducted by an international court.

The hard realists seem at first glance to resemble that unsophisticated and unknowledgeable group isolated in earlier chapters as one of the main sources of unqualified approval of the trial. That the hard realists are as a group relatively unsophisticated and disprivileged seems indeed to be the case. This group tended to be lower class, its members poorly educated and employed in low-prestige occupations.

[2] The method of analysis followed in this chapter differs from that employed throughout most of the book. This has been necessitated, as the technically minded reader will appreciate, by the need to adopt a descriptive rather than an analytic approach where a dependent variable is typological. The effect is to produce a relatively broad portrayal of the dominant characteristics of each type rather than rigorous analysis of determinants.

When it comes to general knowledge of the trial, however, the hard realists are not in a disadvantaged position as compared with the other three types. Hard respondents, who preferred death for Eichmann, were as a group no less knowledgeable than soft respondents, who preferred life imprisonment. If anything, hard realists are distinguished by the greater frequency with which they knew the official estimate of 6 million Jews murdered. It does not appear, therefore, that the hard realists were simply reflecting unknowledgeable and uncritical acceptance of the mass media position on Eichmann's punishment. The explanation for their response would appear to lie in their being least subject to conflicting perspectives in forming their opinions about punishment. Relatively few experienced doubt concerning Eichmann's complicity, the legality of the trial, or Israel's jurisdiction. Finally, a sizable number were aware of the extent of the Nazi atrocities.

It should be recognized that on the whole this was not a particularly sophisticated response. These people, while not especially ignorant of the facts of the trial, were the least exposed to mass media coverage of it. Moreover, being drawn largely from the underprivileged stratum of society, they did not have the capacity for critical assessment that education brings. On the issue of punishment, therefore, as on the other issues that have been discussed, Israel secured its greatest support from the less privileged and sophisticated groups.

The Soft Realists

Predicting a death sentence but personally favoring life imprisonment was the second most frequent response to the punishment issue. Such a response clearly questions the wisdom of the death sentence. The grounds for doing so, however, are not self-evident. Were these people basically sympathetic to the trial and concerned that death was too mild a sentence for Eichmann? Did they feel that he ought to be made to suffer for his crimes and that life imprisonment would be a harsher punishment than death? Were they ignorant of the nature of Eichmann's crimes? Were they using this means to express sympathy for Eichmann? Or was this simply a way to express their general opposition to capital punishment? As with other aspects of the trial, the answer is not simple. A number of elements combined to produce the response of the soft realist.

The soft realists were, if anything, slightly more inclined than hard realists to accept the prosecution's depiction of Eichmann's complicity and guilt. Eighty-four per cent thought of him as a monster or zealot as compared to 76 per cent of the hard realists. This mutual agreement on Eichmann's complicity and guilt was undoubtedly an element in the expectation of death shared by both soft and hard realists. By the same token, however, the personal preference of soft realists for life imprisonment cannot be attributed to their having a "softer" image of Eichmann's complicity and guilt than the hard realists.

What, then, did lead the soft realists personally to reject the court's punishment? More than the hard realists, the soft realists were unsure about the legality of the trial. They were more likely than the hard realists to say they had no opinion on the issue (18 per cent as compared to 6 per cent). And, among those with an opinion, fewer thought that the trial was legal (74 per cent) and unqualifiedly so (45 per cent) than the hard realists, for whom the corresponding figures are 83 per cent and 65 per cent. Moreover, the soft realists were considerably less likely to favor Israel's jurisdiction over the trial when given the alternative of having Eichmann tried by an international court; the proportions favoring Israel's jurisdiction are 32 per cent among the soft realists and 51 per cent among the hard realists. Their greater skepticism regarding the trial's legality did not lead the soft realists to think that the court would take this into account in imposing its sentence. However, in their personal evaluation of the trial, this was a matter to be considered, and their greater concern about legality was apparently one factor in their opposition to the sentence they expected the court to impose.

Disagreement between the two groups is not to be wholly understood, however, as a result of their relatively different perceptions of the trial's legality. Looking further for an explanation, a natural inclination is to search for differences in the two groups' knowledge of the events leading up to the trial. Previous analysis showed that the more knowledgeable respondents were less likely to accept the mass media position on the trial. Perhaps the soft realists were displaying the tendency of the more knowledgeable to disagree with prevailing opinion.

Exploration of this hypothesis does not confirm it. The soft realists scored about as knowledgeable as the hard realists. But the two groups did differ in their knowledge of one issue—the Nazi atrocities toward the Jews. Somewhat fewer of the soft realists (34 per cent) than the hard realists (45 per cent) knew that 6 million Jews had been killed. Thus there was a less compelling reason for the soft realists than for the hard realists to feel that Eichmann deserved death.

Complementing this relative lack of knowledge was what has been interpreted as a concern on the part of the soft realists for the issue of capital punishment. The considerable religiosity exhibited by the soft realists leads one to suspect that capital punishment was a particularly salient issue for them. More than any other group, they reported that religion was very important in their lives. Sixty-eight per cent of the soft realists made this assertion, as compared with 43 per cent of the hard realists.

Presumably one can be religious and countenance capital punishment. Over the centuries capital punishment has been practiced in Western society without being seriously questioned by the churches. In the present climate of opinion, however, people who are religious, perhaps particularly if they interpret the Bible literally, may feel that the Sixth Commandment, "Thou shalt not kill," ought to be taken at its word. The soft realists, aside from being the most religion-conscious of the four groups, were also the most likely to be members of fundamentalist denominations. In addition, because of their religiosity, the soft realists were probably the most likely to have been exposed to the objections of the religious press to the death penalty for Eichmann.

The soft realists' apparent rejection of the death sentence for Eichmann, then, does not seem to have been motivated by a concern that the death sentence would let Eichmann off too easily. Nor were these people adopting this means to show a special sympathy for Eichmann. Rather, what appears to have happened is that a basic reservation about the morality of capital punishment was reinforced by a concern about the legality of the trial and by lack of knowledge and understanding of the Nazi era itself.

This response to the punishment issue was not a particularly sophisticated one. These people, as has already been mentioned, were no more knowledgeable about the events leading up to the trial than were those who both predicted and favored the death penalty. Nor were they more apt to be privileged. They were slightly more likely to be females than the hard realists, a factor associated, perhaps, with their greater religiosity.

The Soft Misperceivers

A third response to the punishment issue was both to favor and to expect a sentence of life imprisonment. It is difficult to interpret this response in terms of its implications for approval or disapproval of the trial. Within their own frame of reference, these people exhibited personal support for what they thought the court's position would be. In this sense, they might be judged as supporting the trial, at least at the time they expressed their opinion on punishment. On the other hand, those who responded in this way were bound to be the most disappointed in the actual outcome of the trial, being frustrated in both preference and expectation.

Earlier comparison of the hard realists with the soft realists was limited to distinguishing between those who preferred death and those who preferred life imprisonment. In trying to understand the soft misperceivers a further complication is introduced. Not only is it necessary to assess the reason that they preferred life imprisonment over death, it is also necessary to assess why they expected life imprisonment instead of death.

The major difference between realists and those who have been called misperceivers is one of privilege and sophistication. Fully 56 per cent of the soft misperceivers were classified as highly privileged or sophisticated compared to only 22 per cent of the hard realists and 26 per cent of the soft realists. These differences are also reflected in the degree to which the three groups report themselves as exposed to information about the trial: 52 per cent of the soft misperceivers scored high on media exposure, as did 41 per cent of the hard realists and 42 per cent of the soft realists.[3]

Since they were more sophisticated, soft misperceivers were uniformly more critical of the trial than hard realists. Among soft misperceivers 21 per cent believed that Eichmann had personally murdered; among hard realists the figure was 33 per cent. Among hard realists 78 per cent thought that the trial was legal; among soft misperceivers, 69

[3] A high score on media exposure is defined as reading or hearing about the trial in three or more different media.

per cent. Among hard realists 51 per cent approved of Israel's jurisdiction; among soft misperceivers, only 28 per cent.

In general, then, the soft misperceivers were people who, while agreeing that Eichmann was guilty, had doubts about the trial. One way of allaying these doubts was to prefer life imprisonment over the more drastic and final penalty of death. But the soft misperceivers went one step further than the soft realists: They apparently believed that the court would share their doubts and also stop short of the death penalty. Their prediction that the court would impose a life sentence might be interpreted as a projection of their own personal reservations concerning the legitimacy of the trial.

Once again, knowledge—at least about Eichmann's capture and identity—is of no greater help in understanding the response of the soft misperceiver than it was in understanding the other responses. The soft misperceivers were, as a group, somewhat less informed than the hard realists about the Nazi atrocities: 38 per cent were informed as compared to 45 per cent of the hard realists. In their knowledge of the atrocities, soft misperceivers resembled soft realists.

That a principled opposition to capital punishment figured in the response of the soft misperceiver is not clear from the superficial evidence. The soft misperceivers were no more religious than the hard realists. They were less religious than the soft realists. Whereas 68 per cent of the soft realists said that religion was important to them, the comparable figure for the soft misperceivers was 41 per cent. These findings indicate that neither their preference for nor their expectation of life imprisonment can be attributed to greater religiosity.

The decision of the soft misperceivers to conclude that the court would impose a sentence of life imprisonment remains an enigma. Their critical attitude toward the trial undoubtedly was an important factor in their personal preference for life imprisonment. But not all respondents who advocated life imprisonment, either out of doubt or out of religious or ethical scruples, actually expected it. The only explanation which suggests itself is that the soft misperceivers, being more sophisticated than the other two groups, were more capable of entertaining the idea that the court would decide on life imprisonment. Since the objectives of the trial were ultimately moral, the more sophisticated might have been convinced that the sentence would itself be a uniquely moral one. This interpretation receives some confirmation in the analysis of the hard misperceivers.

The Hard Misperceivers

Only a handful of people, 11 to be exact, expressed a personal preference for the death penalty at the same time that they expected a court sentence of life imprisonment. Ordinarily, in survey research, no attempt would be made to analyze such a small number of cases. However, out of curiosity, an attempt was made to understand the meaning of this deviant response. The effort was not without reward, for it appears that these people were responding to the punishment issue out of a highly considered assessment of the trial.

Of all four groups, the hard misperceivers were the most critical of the legality of the trial and of the validity of Israel's jurisdiction. At the same time, they were well informed about Eichmann's identity and the Nazi atrocities. Far more than any other group (9 out of 11), the hard misperceivers knew that Eichmann was a Nazi, and they resembled the hard realists in the extent of their knowledge of the Nazi atrocities. Apparently, their belief that Eichmann was guilty as charged and their knowledge of the facts of the persecutions led them personally to favor the death penalty while their misgivings and their sophistication led them to predict a court sentence of life imprisonment.

This interpretation presumes a considerable amount of sophistication on the part of these respondents, and the presumption turned out to be correct. Sixty-three per cent of the hard misperceivers scored as highly privileged. The group was almost exclusively upper or middle class; only one member identified himself as being working class. The hard misperceivers were high in their reported exposure to the mass media and were generally knowledgeable: All correctly answered at least two of the four knowledge questions asked in the interview.

Their personal support of the death sentence for Eichmann suggests that opposition to capital punishment was not particularly salient for the hard misperceivers. Only two considered religion to be very important in their lives. Of all four groups, this one was by far the least religious.

It seems reasonable to conclude that the hard misperceivers were the most discriminating of the four groups in their observations of the trial. These people were sophisticated enough to sense the ambiguity in Israel's claim to jurisdiction. At the same time they were sympathetic to and knowledgeable about the motives that had led to Israel's prosecution of Eichmann. Despite their misgivings the hard misperceivers seemed to have arrived at their preference for the death sentence because of a fuller awareness of the issues involved. While it is true that their position was an ambiguous one, it seems evident that the hard misperceivers had the sophistication to separate the trial's means from its ultimate objectives. Their criticism did not interfere with their conviction that Eichmann deserved the sentence of death. However, their sophistication led them to believe that the court would be lenient in the interests of achieving its moral objectives.

The Negro Response

Negroes, it will be recalled, were less likely than whites to be aware of the trial; and, among those who were aware, fewer Negroes than whites had an opinion on Eichmann's guilt. Of 141 Negroes in the sample, only 93 were aware of the trial, and of those only 43 had opinions on both questions concerning Eichmann's guilt. Consequently only 43 Negroes were eligible to comment on Eichmann's punishment.

Compared to the whites, Negroes with an opinion were somewhat less inclined (49 per cent as against 55 per cent) to expect a court sentence of death and were even relatively more uninclined personally to favor the death sentence (18 per cent as compared to 37 per cent). The predominant response among Negroes was both to expect and to favor a sentence of life imprisonment (36 per cent gave this response); the predominant response among whites was to expect and favor the death sentence (28 per cent).

This over-all proclivity on the Negroes' part to be more lenient is manifested in all segments of the Negro population, and cannot be explained by differences between Negroes and whites in background characteristics or in their knowledge about and attitudes toward the trial. Such differences clearly exist, of course, as has been shown throughout the earlier analysis. However, holding them constant, the Negro is always more lenient on the punishment issue than his white counterpart.

This is quite the opposite of what might have been expected. The less privileged white person, it will be recalled, was less inclined to be lenient on punishment than the more privileged one. Consequently, it might reasonably have been predicted that the Negro, whose deprivation on the average is more severe, would have exhibited the least leniency of any group. The fact that this is not the case suggests that there is something distinctive in the situation of the Negro which contributes to this unexpected result.

The data do not provide any direct evidence as to what this distinctive feature might be. It is suspected, however, that the explanation does not lie in the Negro's response to the trial per se, but rather in the special significance that the death penalty may hold for him. For the average white person, the possibility of his knowing anyone or of his personally being involved in a situation where the death sentence may be an issue is remote indeed. With the higher crime rate in the Negro community and with one hundred years' experience of the white man's justice behind him, the possibility may not be so remote for the Negro. Conceivably, his response to the questions on Eichmann's punishment may very well have been influenced by the greater salience of the punishment issue for him.

It is possible, moreover, that Negroes are more sensitive than whites to the possibilities of a miscarriage of justice. Consequently, in the present case, Negroes may have been more hesitant about wanting the death penalty imposed. While this may explain the general propensity of Negroes to be more lenient than whites in their preferences, it does not explain their tendency to expect life imprisonment as well. Nor does it account for the variations in Negro response. Not all Negroes expected and favored a sentence of life imprisonment. Of the 43 Negroes who were asked about punishment, 7 were hard realists (both favoring and expecting the death penalty for Eichmann); 12 were soft realists (expecting the death penalty but not personally supporting it); 15 were soft misperceivers (both preferring and predicting life imprisonment); none were hard misperceivers (preferring death while expecting life): Six reported they had no opinion on one or both questions; and 3 gave some other response on one or both questions.

The small number of cases makes systematic analysis of the Negro data impossible. Several tendencies were sufficiently marked, however, to warrant being reported. Among the hard realists, there was a greater disposition to see the trial as legal, to favor Israel's jurisdiction, and to accept the prosecution's portrayal of Eichmann's complicity than among the other groups. In these respects, the data roughly parallel the white data. As among the whites, the soft realists tended to be the most religious. The tendency, noted earlier, for the more privileged Negroes to be more receptive to Israel's position on the trial issues is also repeated here. Thus, unlike whites, Negroes who were hard realists tended to be drawn from the more privileged rather than the less privileged strata. Similarly, in distinction to the white community, Negroes who were soft realists were more rather than less privileged compared to soft misperceivers.

It is perhaps of special significance that no Negroes predicted a court punishment of life while personally favoring the death penalty. This was the response of a small but highly sophisticated and privileged group in the white community. While this degree of privilege and sophistication exists in the Negro community, it is too infrequent to be picked up in a sample of the size interviewed.

Summary and Conclusions

The central finding of the analysis of opinions on Eichmann's punishment is that, once again, level of sophistication or privilege played a major role. The most consistent and largest difference between realists and misperceivers is their level of sophistication: As a group misperceivers are far more sophisticated than realists. That an inaccurate prediction of the court sentence is highly associated with sophistication is another of the paradoxical findings of this study. In this case no resolution can be found in the data. The most plausible explanation, perhaps, is that their very sophistication led some people to imagine that the court would refrain from imposing the obvious penalty of death, either because the court shared their misgivings concerning the trial or because the court wished to mete out a "higher justice" consonant with the "higher morality" of the trial. Whatever the reason, however, misjudging the outcome of the trial cannot be attributed to lack of sophistication.

Most misperceivers also voiced a preference for life imprisonment. Only 11 white respondents were hard misperceivers, that is, preferring the death penalty even though they predicted life imprisonment. Three important differences distinguished hard from soft misperceivers. Hard misperceivers were highly unlikely to be religious. They were more apt to be aware of the Nazi atrocities. As a group, they were even more sophisticated than the generally sophisticated soft misperceivers. More than any other group, the hard misperceivers were torn between their strong criticism of the trial and their knowledge of the atrocities. But, if their extremely high level of sophistication made them aware both of the ambiguities of Israel's actions and of the atrocities, that same sophistication led them to a position that was essentially supportive of the trial.

Realists were on the whole unsophisticated. This is true of both hard realists and soft realists. But the hard realists were less likely to be religious and somewhat more likely to be informed about the atrocities. As between hard and soft realists, the primary difference appears to lie in the considerably greater religiosity of the latter. Of all groups, the soft realists were by far the most religious.

Despite the strong influence of sophistication, general

knowledgeability had no apparent influence on opinions concerning Eichmann's punishment. What mattered was whether one had accurate knowledge of the number of Jews killed by the Nazis. Whether the respondent predicted a court sentence of life imprisonment or a court sentence of death, a personal preference for the death penalty was associated with accurate knowledge of the extent of the Nazi atrocities.

The fact that general knowledgeability concerning the trial did not influence opinion on Eichmann's punishment suggests that, when it came to deciding this issue, extraneous considerations having little to do with the trial entered into the decision. On the issue of Eichmann's complicity and guilt, as well as the legality of the trial, level of general knowledgeability concerning the trial did have an influence: The higher the level of knowledgeability, the more the tendency of respondents to be critical. But general knowledgeability concerning the trial did not influence respondents to prefer one sentence over the other. Apparently their preferences were based not on how much they had learned about the events of the trial but on other considerations.

One of these considerations was religion: It may well have been the case that the more religious were influenced by the widespread opposition of the Protestant religious press to the death penalty. But another consideration was specific knowledge of the atrocities. Just as religiosity made for a preference for life imprisonment, so accurate knowledge of the atrocities made for a preference for the death penalty.

All in all, white respondents showed a general tendency to be lenient either in preference or in prediction. Only 28 per cent of the white awares who could be classified on punishment were hard realists. Thus, only about a quarter were convinced that death was the proper and forthcoming penalty. This finding should not be interpreted as a measure of hostility to the trial. To the extent that extraneous factors such as religiosity entered, attitudes of leniency had little to do with the trial itself. However, it is possible that Ben-Gurion's defense of the "higher morality" of the trial produced a boomerang effect. It might have done so by creating an erroneous impression among the sophisticated that the court would give concrete expression to this higher morality by a sentence of life imprisonment.

If the white respondents tended to be lenient, Negro respondents tended to be even more so. While white hard realists were in the minority, they were nevertheless the largest single group among whites. Among Negroes, the largest single group were the soft misperceivers who constituted 35 per cent of those with opinions on punishment. What is still more striking is that among whites hard realists were unsophisticated while among Negroes the opposite was the case: Hard realists were more sophisticated than soft misperceivers.

It is conjectured that the lenient response of the unsophisticated Negroes—who are, of course, the most disprivileged members of the society—reflects their general attitudes toward the legal system rather than hostility toward the trial. Conversely, the more punitive response of the more sophisticated Negro reflects his acceptance of the prevailing legal norms.

The feelings evoked by the punishment issue were apparently not a reflection of prejudice either in the white or the Negro community. However the data are examined, there is no evidence that prejudice, except for a handful of people, was a ground on which responses were based.

CHAPTER 6

IMPACT OF THE TRIAL

THE manifest purpose of the Eichmann trial was to bring a criminal to justice. But the trial was also conceived as a means of combating anti-Semitism. However painful to the survivors, a recapitulation of the unspeakable horrors suffered by the Jews would be a reminder to non-Jews everywhere of the continuing need to struggle against all manifestations of anti-Semitism, whether passive, polite, or rabid. Not only would the facts of Jewish suffering serve to justify Israel's capture of Eichmann, they would create a reservoir of sympathy for the Jewish people as a whole.

The mass media, even when they had reservations about Israel's handling of the trial, had no such qualms about the validity of its educational aims. Much of the trial was given over to documenting the facts of the "final solution," and the mass media reported, sympathetically and in detail, the many eyewitness accounts of Nazi depravity introduced into evidence. Editorial opinion, too, was sympathetic; and during the course of the trial, almost all the mass media, local as well as national, took occasion to underline their concern that the trial accomplish its long-range educational purposes.

It is open to question, however, whether Israel, the mass media, and responsible citizens everywhere were not guilty of wishful thinking in harboring the hope that the trial could accomplish its ultimate goals. The Nazi horrors, when they occurred, had failed to stir the conscience of a passive and indifferent world. The chance that a recapitulation of the horrors would succeed where the horrors themselves had failed seems rather remote indeed. Yet the very viability of the trial as an educational instrument rested on this premise. To what extent was it warranted?

Not only past experience, but the data of the present study indicate that the educational message of the trial could not in any case have reached all of the Oakland public. At the time of the interview, 16 per cent of the Oakland public was not even aware that the trial was taking place. Moreover, analysis revealed that, precisely because it was a serious news event, the Eichmann trial was largely ignored by that section of the American public whose major interest is in nonserious news. Nothing in the data suggests that the Eichmann trial was singled out for special attention; those who were well informed on the trial consisted of that handful of people who ordinarily and routinely attend to serious events, whatever their nature. If paying close attention to the trial was a necessary condition for grasping and internalizing its message, there is good reason to doubt that the educational aims of the trial were accomplished to a significant degree. The viability of these aims becomes further suspect when it is remembered that those people who did pay attention to the trial were likely to be critical of the way it was handled.

While the grounds for pessimism seem overwhelming, it is also true that critics of the trial were in a minority. Most people were favorably disposed to the prosecution's case against Eichmann and to the legality of the trial. The relative absence of criticism in the general public may, of course, merely reflect the apathy with which the trial tended to be viewed. One cannot be sure, however, and the possibility remains that people's hearts were touched by the message of the trial even though its factual details were not impressed on their minds. It is also possible that criticisms of the trial did not blind people to its message.

In order to test these possibilities, three questions are explored. First, to what extent did the public view the trial as, in the end, a good thing? The public had its criticisms and misgivings, but did this lead them to reject the trial as a whole? Second, how much understanding of the scope and extent of the Nazi atrocities did the trial convey? Many people underestimated the size of the official estimate of the number of million Jews killed, but did this reflect a mere lapse of memory or some unconscious attempt to reject the facts? Third, to what extent did the public feel greater sympathy for the Jewish people as a consequence of the trial?

Differences in the responses of whites and Negroes again make it necessary to consider them separately in the analysis. The results reported below are for whites only; comparative material on Negroes is presented later.

General Acceptance of the Trial

After being queried on the details of the trial, respondents were asked: Do you think it was a good thing that Eichmann was brought to trial, or not so good? The danger that the trial would have a boomerang effect was always present, and the answers to this question provide a clue to the extent, if any, to which it occurred. Judging from the results, the effect, while present, was minor. Most respondents were disposed to feel that it was a good thing that Eichmann had been brought to trial; 77 per cent of the white respondents who were aware of the trial gave this response. Of the remainder, 15 per cent replied in the negative, and 8 per cent said they did not know. Fifteen per cent seems a small number; in the sample this represented only 42 people. Projecting this proportion to the white population of Oakland, however, results in a figure of

45,000 people who could be said to have disapproved of the trial. Viewed in these terms, the number appears more significant, and an inquiry into who these people were and what motivated their responses seems in order.

As might be expected, those who disapproved of the trial were much more critical of Israel's handling of the trial than those who approved. For example, 43 per cent of the disapprovers viewed the trial as definitely illegal as compared to only 11 per cent of the approvers. Among disapprovers only 52 per cent judged Eichmann to be guilty; among approvers, 85 per cent. A substantial majority of the approvers thought of Eichmann as a monster or a zealot; among disapprovers the dominant image was that of acquiescent bureaucrat.

In view of the propensity for the knowledgeable and sophisticated to be critical of Israel's handling of the trial, it is not surprising that, by and large, disapprovers were more sophisticated and knowledgeable than approvers. Among approvers, 36 per cent were able to answer three or four of the knowledge questions correctly; 62 per cent of the disapprovers were able to do so. On all five indicators used to construct the index of sophistication (or privilege), disapprovers were consistently more likely to possess high-status characteristics. They were more likely to be male, to have a good education, to be a homeowner, to have a high income, and to hold a more prestigious job. As Table 35 shows, the proportion saying that the trial was a good thing declines with each step up the sophistication ladder. Note, for example, that 100 per cent of the least sophisticated with an opinion said that the Eichmann trial was a good thing. Among the most sophisticated, about two-thirds made this final positive evaluation of the trial.

The influence of anti-Semitism on respondents' over-all evaluation of the trial appears, on the whole, to have been negligible. Indeed, on the general index of anti-Semitism, approvers (39 per cent) were slightly more likely than disapprovers (34 per cent) to score as anti-Semitic. The discrimination index produces no difference: 18 per cent of the approvers and 17 per cent of the disapprovers scored as

TABLE 35. APPROVAL OF TRIAL BY LEVEL OF SOPHISTICATION
(white respondents only)

Reply to: *"Do You Think It Was a Good Thing That Eichmann Was Brought to Trial or Not So Good?"*	*Level of Sophistication*					
	Low 0	1	2	3	4	High 5
Good thing	100%	90%	89%	85%	79%	62%
Not so good	0	10	11	15	21	38
Number with an opinion	(10)	(51)	(54)	(47)	(62)	(29)
Don't know	17%	7%	7%	11%	3%	6%
Total number	(12)	(55)	(58)	(53)	(64)	(31)

discriminatory. On the third measure of anti-Semitism, the relation was reversed. Disapprovers were slightly more likely to segregate themselves from Jews; the figures are 48 per cent for disapprovers and 40 per cent for approvers. Further analysis, holding sophistication and knowledge constant, confirms the conclusion that anti-Semitism was not a major factor influencing response to the question on whether the Eichmann trial was a good thing.

The process revealed by these results is one that begins with the more sophisticated person being led to greater exposure and greater knowledge of the trial proceedings. Knowledge, together perhaps with awareness of elite commentary on the trial, bred a critical stance toward the way the trial was handled. This in turn contributed to more negative over-all evaluations of the trial.

Perhaps the most significant result is that the vast majority of respondents made a positive over-all evaluation of the trial. One way of formulating this is to note that over-all approval of the trial was greater than approval of its specific details. Of the white respondents who were aware of the trial, 77 per cent thought it was a good thing. This is a higher figure than the proportion thinking that the trial was legal (56 per cent), or the proportion accepting the prosecution's depiction of Eichmann's complicity and guilt (48 per cent), or the proportion who both expected and approved the death sentence for Eichmann (28 per cent). Some people were evidently able to transcend their criticism of the details of the trial and come to an over-all positive evaluation.

While it is reassuring that a majority, even a substantial one, viewed the trial as a whole in positive terms, there remains the question of the significance of this finding. Did people take this view because they were deeply moved by the trial's message? Or was the response an essentially superficial one, reflecting lack of attention to the trial and automatic acceptance of the position of a sympathetic press? Clearly, more stringent criteria have to be met before one can feel sanguine about the trial's impact.

Response to the Nazi Atrocities

It remains today a disquieting fact that world opinion was not uniformly outraged by the Nazi crimes against the Jews. Examination of opinion polls conducted in the United States during that time conveys the impression that by and large Americans were not deeply touched by the news from Nazi Germany. To some extent people were simply unable to believe that such horrors were in fact taking place.[1] Present

[1] In January 1943, only 47 per cent of a nationally representative sample believed reports that 2 million Jews had been killed in Europe since the war. Twenty-nine per cent indicated that they thought the news was only rumor. The remaining 24 per cent had no opinion [Hadley Cantril (ed.), *Public Opinion 1935–1946* (Princeton: Princeton University Press, 1951), p. 383].

too was sheer indifference: What was going on in Europe was none of America's business.

Since the end of World War II, there have been several occasions for presenting to the world incontrovertible evidence of the extent and horror of the Nazi atrocities. Any lingering doubts that the Nazi persecution of the Jews was exaggerated were quickly dissipated with the end of the war as the evidence became directly accessible to investigation. At that time, the results of the investigation were widely reported in the world's press and in films of the concentration camps, the gas chambers, the mass burial grounds, and the pitiful condition of the few survivors.

The Nuremberg trials of 1945–1949 served once more to remind the world of what had occurred, and to do so with all the authority that an international tribunal commands. The facts were again given wide publicity, and the estimate that 6 million Jews were killed was given official status on the basis of Nazi records. Until the Eichmann trial, no other occasion presented itself to communicate on a worldwide scale what the Nazis had done. The task was, in effect, turned over to the world's classrooms.

By the time of the Eichmann trial, the generation that had lived through World War II was middle-aged and more. A large proportion of the world's population was represented by those who were children or as yet unborn during the Nazi era. The trial shared in part the audience that had been exposed to the war and to the Nuremburg trials. But it was also a vehicle for reaching those who were at the time too young to have been informed by these earlier events. Thus, the trial provided a unique opportunity to re-educate an older generation and to educate a newer one in the cruelties of which man is capable.

How well did it succeed? It is impossible to say how many Oaklanders were led to a better comprehension of the Nazi atrocities because of the Eichmann trial. However, it *is* possible to say that, by the time the trial proceedings were over, there was still a substantial segment of the public who thought that the Nazi persecutions were partly or mostly the Jews' own fault and who contended that the official estimate of the number of Jews killed was inflated.

The question asked in the interview concerning the degree to which the Jews were responsible for their fate was similar to one used in previous surveys. It read "Thinking back to the treatment of the Jews by Nazi Germany *before and during* World War II, do you think the persecution of the Jews was mostly their own fault, partly their own fault, or not at all their own fault?"[2] Once again, only respondents aware of the trial were asked the question. Of these, 53 per cent said that the Nazi persecutions were not at all the Jews' fault. But 30 per cent said they were partly the Jews' fault, and 2 per cent said they were mostly the Jews' fault. The remainder, 15 per cent, did not know.

To find, after the trial, that as many as 47 per cent of the American public either had no opinion or still believed the Jews to be partly or mostly to blame for the unmitigated horrors that befell them is disturbing indeed. A reading of the interviews shows that some respondents meant that the Jews were at fault in the sense that they should have been more aggressive in opposing their persecutors. But that more respondents interpreted the question as it was intended—as indicating that the Jews were somehow responsible for their persecution—is suggested by the results presented in Table 36. This table shows that how one answered the question on

[2] In April 1938, Gallup included the following question in a national poll: "Do you think that the persecution of the Jews in Europe has been their own fault?" Only 31 per cent thought that the Jews were not at all to blame. Forty-eight per cent indicated that the Jews were partly at fault, and 10 per cent were willing to cast the entire blame on the Jews. The remaining 11 per cent had no opinion or did not answer the question (*ibid.*, p. 381).

fault had some influence on one's over-all evaluation of the trial, particularly among the five respondents who thought that the Jews were mostly at fault.

There is more reliable evidence, however, that the trial

TABLE 36. APPROVAL OF TRIAL BY VIEW OF JEWISH RESPONSIBILITY FOR NAZI PERSECUTION (white respondents only)

Reply to: "*Do you think it was a good thing that Eichmann was brought to trial or not so good?*"	Reply to: "*Thinking back to the treatment of the Jews by Nazi Germany* before and during *World War II, do you think the persecution of the Jews was mostly their own fault, partly their own fault, or not at all their own fault?*"			
	Mostly[a]	Partly	Not at All	Don't Know
Good thing	(2)	78%	87%	88%
Not so good	(3)	22	13	12
Number with an opinion	(5)	(76)	(140)	(34)
Don't know	0	8%	5%	17%
Total number	(5)	(83)	(147)	(41)

[a] Because of the small number of cases no percentages are reported.

failed to overcome the abiding propensity of many people not to face up to the reality of the Nazi horrors and indeed to exhibit some wish to explain them away. This is provided by two questions concerning the official estimate of 6 million Jews killed by the Nazis. Throughout the entire trial proceedings, probably the single piece of information about the Nazi period most often repeated in the mass media was the fact that 6 million Jews had been annihilated. At a bare minimum, it would seem that the trial, if it was to succeed at all, had to communicate this simple fact. Yet as has already been shown in Chapter 2, by the time the trial proceedings had ended, only 33 per cent of Oaklanders aware of the trial were able to say that the official estimate was 6 million. As Table 37 shows, the figure for whites is 36 per cent. This ignorance looms larger when it is remembered that information about the official estimate had been circulating for a long time before the trial began.

Communicating the official estimate is one thing; persuading people to accept it is another. In order to measure

TABLE 37. KNOWLEDGE OF THE OFFICIAL ESTIMATE OF JEWS KILLED BY THE NAZIS
(white respondents only)

Official Estimate Was	Aware of the Trial
Correct answer: 6,000,000	36%
Incorrect answers:	
10,000 or less	3
100,000	4
500,000	5
1,000,000	9
2,000,000	9
4,000,000	12
8,000,000	6
10,000,000	7
Total incorrect answers	55%
Don't know	9
Number	(276)

both knowledge and acceptance the following sequence of questions was presented. Respondents were first asked what the official estimate actually was and were given a list of figures from which to choose. After they had given a figure, respondents were told that the official estimate was 6 million. They were then asked whether they thought this was too high, about right, or too low. If the answer was "too high" or "too low," the respondent was given the same list of figures that he had been given before and asked, "What do you think is the real number?"

On the basis of their response to the first question, asking for the actual official estimate, respondents can be divided into four groups: "gross underestimators" (those who guessed 2 million or less), "moderate underestimators" (those who said 4 million), those who gave the right answer, and "over-estimators." Table 38 shows that there is a strong relation between the respondent's own version of the official estimate and his acceptance of the correct estimate.[3] Looking first at

TABLE 38. ACCEPTANCE OF OFFICIAL ESTIMATE BY KNOWLEDGE OF OFFICIAL ESTIMATE
(white respondents only)

	Initial Choice of Official Estimate				
Personal Estimate	6,000,000	2,000,000 or Less	4,000,000	More Than 6,000,000	*Total*[b]
Correct answer:					
6,000,000	54%	24%	41%	50%	40%
Incorrect answers:					
2,000,000 or less	10	40	15	0	18
4,000,000	2	6	18	0	6
More than 6,000,000	4	1	0	25	5
Don't know	30	29	26	25	31
Number	(100)	(82)	(34)	(36)	(276)

[a] Percentages show proportion of respondents who gave estimate of number of Jews killed by Nazis during World War II (figures listed in left-hand column) after making a choice among figures listed along top of table and then being told the official estimate of the number of Jews killed.

[b] Includes twenty-four respondents who answered "don't know" on official estimate.

the gross underestimators, only 24 per cent accepted the official estimate after being told what it was. Almost half gave personal estimates of 2 million or less, that is, they gave personal estimates in line with their earlier reply on official estimate. One explanation of this tendency on the part of the gross underestimators is that, having made a wild guess at the

[3] In this table, 24 respondents who did not offer a figure for the official estimate are omitted from the calculations. It can be remarked in passing that 58 per cent of this group refused or were unable to give a personal estimate. Of the remainder, 21 per cent accepted the official estimate. But 13 per cent and 8 per cent gave personal estimates, respectively, of 4 million and 2 million or less. Thus, whatever their reasons, 21 per cent of this group, after being told that the official estimate was 6 million, felt that it was too high.

official estimate, they sought to save face by making a congruent personal estimate.[4] While face-saving is a plausible explanation of the responses, it is not possible to dismiss the view that some of the underestimators actually believed the official estimates to be exaggerated. In fact, their original underestimation of the official figure may in some cases have represented "wishful thinking."

The moderate underestimators who gave the official estimate as 4 million were closer to the truth than the gross underestimators. Perhaps this is the reason that considerably more (41 per cent) were willing to accept the official figure of 6 million. Only a few (18 per cent) gave personal estimates congruent with their earlier guess of 4 million. But 15 per cent gave personal estimates of less than 2 million. Presumably these are people who were going beyond face-saving to self-conscious rejection of the official estimate.

If moderate underestimators were more willing to accept the official estimate than gross underestimators, the group that originally gave the correct figure were still more willing to accept it. Here 54 per cent accepted it, and an additional 4 per cent thought that the actual number of Jews killed was more than 6 million. But 12 per cent agreed with the misinformed that the figure of 6 million was too high.

Among overestimators not a single person gave a personal estimate of less than 6 million. Furthermore, 25 per cent gave personal estimates congruent with their original figure for the official estimate. The pattern of responses for overestimators reveals clearly the defensive posture of the misinformed. Those who overestimated could have accepted the official estimate without losing face; yet after being informed of the actual figure, a sizable minority stuck to their guns.

[4] This group did not, incidentally, overselect the "don't know" response when asked to give a personal estimate. The proportion of "don't know" responses on personal estimate was about 29 per cent irrespective of the respondent's answer to the question on official estimate.

The pattern of the overestimators suggests that some unknown portion of the sample refused to accept the figure of 6 million simply because they wished to defend an erroneous guess. There must also have been some who accepted it without having real convictions on the matter. Although the results cannot be interpreted as a precise reflection of the actual proportions of Oaklanders who self-consciously and with conviction accepted or rejected the official estimate of 6 million, they do reveal something about the lack of understanding the public has of the extent of the Nazi atrocities. Despite a year of headlines and constant reiteration of the official estimate, 51 per cent of the white respondents aware of the trial either underestimated or did not know the correct figure. After being told the correct figure, 55 per cent of the white sample rejected it as inflated or refused to commit themselves on its accuracy. These results may be partially understandable in terms of the simple inability of many people to remember numbers or to comprehend large magnitudes.[5] Nevertheless, whatever their reasons for replying as they did, it is safe to say that a good part of the Oakland adult population is either unable to comprehend or unwilling to admit the extent of the Nazi atrocities. On this criterion, the trial failed to reach and educate a substantial segment of the public.

What accounts for these results? First, why did the trial largely fail to convey the one fact that symbolized its central message concerning the demonic potentialities of anti-Semitism? Knowledge of the official estimate, like being generally informed, is related to the level of sophistication. The more sophisticated are the more likely to know the official estimate (Table 39). Furthermore, knowing the official estimate

[5] Analysis of the data showed a correlation between level of education and size of estimate. The very lowest estimates were given only by those with least education; as education increased, "lowest" estimate also increased until, at the college level, no person gave an estimate of less than 2 million.

is highly related to being informed about other aspects of the trial. For example, among those who answered the other three questions correctly, 63 per cent also knew the official estimate. At the other extreme, 12 per cent knew the official

TABLE 39. KNOWLEDGE OF OFFICIAL ESTIMATE BY LEVEL OF PRIVILEGE (white respondents only)

Knowledge of Official Estimate	*Level of Sophistication* Low 0	1	2	3	4	High 5
Correct answer:						
6,000,000	25%	29%	33%	36%	39%	58%
Incorrect answers:						
Less than 2,000,000	8	27	34	41	25	22
4,000,000	25	8	10	15	16	10
More than 6,000,000	25	18	9	6	17	10
Don't know	17	18	14	2	3	0
Number	(12)	(55)	(58)	(53)	(64)	(31)

estimate among those who did not know the correct answer to any of the three other questions. People who were generally unknowledgeable not only guessed more when they gave the official estimate, but the less people knew, the wider their guesses. Among the least knowledgeable, 21 per cent guessed that the official estimate was five hundred thousand or less; the equivalent figure for the most knowledgeable is 7 per cent.

Focusing for the moment on the 100 white respondents who gave the correct figure of 6 million, 17 per cent rejected the estimate as inflated.[6] In view of the very small number of rejecters it is not possible to pursue analysis far. However, when rejecters are compared with accepters, consistent differences appear. As Table 40 shows, rejecters were less sophisticated than accepters (29 per cent versus 46 per cent). They were also less generally knowledgeable (59 per cent versus

[6] Of these 17 people, only 12 then went on to report a personal estimate, as may be noted in Table 38.

80 per cent). Surprisingly, however, despite their relatively lower sophistication and knowledgeability, the rejecters were more critical of the trial. They were more likely to consider

TABLE 40. CHARACTERISTICS OF INFORMED ACCEPTERS AND REJECTERS OF THE OFFICIAL ESTIMATE[a]
(white respondents only)

	Rejectors	Accepters
Highly sophisticated	29%	46%
Knowledgeable	59	80
Judging trial illegal	47	37
Anti-Semitic:		
General index	44	38
Discrimination index	24	19
Self-segregation index	59	42
Number	(17)	(59)

[a] These respondents knew the official estimate of the number of Jews killed by the Nazis prior to the interview. The 24 respondents who answered "dont' know" on official estimate are again omitted.

the trial illegal (47 per cent versus 37 per cent). These results contradict the general tenor of earlier findings that the more sophisticated and knowledgeable were the more prone to be critical. What they suggest is that acceptance of the official estimate among the sophisticated tempered their criticism of the trial whereas rejection of the estimate among the unsophisticated increased criticism.[7] Rejecters were slightly but consistently more likely to score as anti-Semitic. The figures are 44 per cent versus 38 per cent on the general index, 24 per cent versus 19 per cent on the discrimination index, and 59 per cent versus 42 per cent on the self-segregation measure.

The picture that emerges from this limited analysis is that outright rejection of the official estimate when one had knowledge of it was an infrequent response. There were only 17 rejecters. Nevertheless, rejection was associated with being

[7] This speculation is supported by additional evidence to be presented later in this chapter.

critical of Israel's handling of the trial and with a certain degree of anti-Semitism.

Informing the misinformed[8] of the correct figure, and then asking them whether or not they accepted it, is obviously different from asking the same question of those who knew the estimate beforehand. Of the 152 white respondents who were misinformed on the official estimate, 36 per cent accepted the information supplied by the interviewer, agreeing that the official estimate was correct. Of the remainder, 41 per cent continued to assert that the figure was other than 6 million, and 23 per cent said they did not know.

The most striking difference between the informed and the misinformed was that, among the misinformed, rejecters were more rather than less likely than accepters to be sophisticated and to be knowledgeable (Table 41). In both groups, how-

TABLE 41. CHARACTERISTICS OF MISINFORMED ACCEPTERS AND REJECTERS OF THE OFFICIAL ESTIMATE[a]
(white respondents only)

	Rejectors	Accepters
Highly sophisticated	35%	27%
Knowledgeable	18	11
Judging trial illegal	24	14
Anti-Semitic:		
General index	40	25
Discrimination index	27	11
Self-segregation index	47	39
Number	(55)	(62)

[a] These respondents had not known the official estimate of the number of Jews killed by the Nazis prior to the interview.

[8] The misinformed include both the underestimators and the overestimators but exclude the uninformed, that is, the "don't knows." It will be recalled that there were 24 "don't knows" and that 58 per cent did not give a personal estimate. Consequently, they are omitted from further analysis. The decision to combine the underestimators and the overestimators was based on the finding that the two groups were composed of the same kinds of people. Overestimators apparently were guessing as much as the underestimators.

ever, rejecters were more apt to see the trial as illegal and to score as anti-Semitic on all three measures.

These results appear to contradict the conclusion of previous chapters in two respects. First, in the earlier analysis, one of the more significant findings was that being informed and being sophisticated was conducive to being critical of the way the trial was handled. Now it is found (Table 38) that being knowledgeable concerning the official estimate of the number of Jews killed by the Nazis is highly conducive to accepting the estimate, that is, to being uncritical. This difficulty is easily resolved by the data. Table 42 shows that

TABLE 42. VIEW OF THE TRIAL'S LEGALITY BY KNOWLEDGE AND ACCEPTANCE OF OFFICIAL ESTIMATE
(white respondents only)

Per Cent Judging Trial as Legal[a]:	*Knowledge of Official Estimate* Correct	Incorrect or Don't Know
Reject official estimate[b]	47%	74%
Number	(15)	(57)
Accept official estimate	58%	83%
Number	(52)	(58)

[a] The "don't knows" on legality have been omitted from this table. The four cells are as follows:

	Correct	*Don't Know*
Reject	12% (17)	10% (63)
Accept	12% (59)	13% (67)

[b] The "don't knows" on acceptance are not included in this table.

those who correctly gave the official estimate were indeed more critical than the misinformed and uninformed when it came to saying that the trial was illegal. However, among both those who knew and those who did not know the official estimate, those who accepted it were less critical than those who rejected it. Thus, while knowledgeability made for a strong tendency to be critical of the trial, this tendency was somewhat reduced when the individual accepted the official estimate.

Less easily explained is a second anomaly. Earlier it was shown that anti-Semitism did not have a consistent or important bearing on the way people responded to Israel's handling of the trial. Anti-Semitism is now found to be consistently related to whether or not respondents accepted the official estimate of the Nazi atrocities. Why this should occur in the one case and not in the other is not clear. Unfortunately, the data provide no clue to the resolution of the apparent contradiction.

Conceivably the explanation lies in the peculiar salience of the official estimate to the anti-Semitic person, a salience not shared by the trial as a whole. Because of the generally low level of knowledge exhibited about the Eichmann trial it was concluded that the trial was not a highly salient issue for the public, and therefore did not engage its anti-Semitic feelings. It is probably incorrect, however, to infer from the widespread lack of accurate knowledge of the official estimate that it, too, is nonsalient. Widespread underestimation of the official estimate may reflect a desire to avoid acknowledging the magnitude of the actual figure. Since disbelief of the official estimate has long been part of the arsenal of the professional anti-Semite, it is not surprising that rejection of the figure should show some association with anti-Semitism.

Sympathy for the Jews

The final criterion on which the net impact of the trial may be judged is its success in winning increased sympathy for the Jewish people and for Israel. What place the trial eventually occupies in history is likely to be determined not by whether the world was persuaded of the wisdom of Israel's actions but by whether it was persuaded that the Nazi horrors should never be allowed to repeat themselves.

Table 43 reports the distribution of answers to two questions: "Has the Eichmann trial made you feel more sympathetic or less sympathetic toward the Jews?" "Has the Eichmann trial made you feel more sympathetic or less sym-

TABLE 43. EFFECT OF TRIAL ON ATTITUDE TOWARD JEWS AND ISRAEL[a]
(white respondents only)

Reply to: *"Has the Eichmann Trial Made You Feel More or Less Sympathetic Toward Israel?"*	Reply to: *"Has the Eichmann Trial Made You Feel More or Less Sympathetic to Jews?"*				
	More	Less	Same	Don't Know	Total
More	29%	1%	3%	1%	34%
Less	1	1	4	1	7
Same	6		48	1	55
Don't Know	1		2	1	4
Total	37%	2%	57%	4%	100%

[a] All percentages are based on the total number of white awares (276).

pathetic toward Israel?" A much larger proportion of respondents, 37 per cent as against 2 per cent, said that the trial made them feel more rather than less sympathetic toward Jews. The ratio of favorable responses was about the same for Israel: 34 per cent as against 7 per cent. While the alternative of saying "about the same" was not included in the question, 57 per cent volunteered this response with respect to the Jews, 55 per cent with respect to Israel.[9]

Responses to the two questions are highly correlated. Giving one response to the question about the Jews was tantamount to giving the same response to the question on Israel. There was a slightly greater positive reaction in answer to the question asked about the Jewish people, but the difference is negligible. Further analysis will concentrate only on the response to the question about Jews.

On the positive side, the results indicate once again that

[9] The Gallup poll of June 1961 asked: "Has the Eichmann trial made you feel more sympathetic or less sympathetic toward Israel and the Jewish people?" The national results for white Christians are similar to those of the Oakland study: 34 per cent replied "more sympathetic"; 5 per cent, "less sympathetic"; 46 per cent, "no difference"; and 15 per cent had no opinion (Crespi, *op. cit.*, p. 95).

the trial did not produce a significant boomerang or negative effect. Moreover, in view of the perennial difficulty of engaging the public in issues they do not perceive as of direct personal concern, the fact that more than one-third of the public was moved to express greater sympathy would appear to constitute a relative success. On the negative side is the fact that a majority of the public said that the trial had no effect on their feelings either way. This result reinforces the tenor of earlier findings that by and large the public was only passively involved in the trial and in what it was seeking to accomplish.

Before such a conclusion can be firmly stated, it is necessary to explore the meaning of saying that one's sympathy toward the Jews stayed the same despite the trial. It may mean that one was already so favorably disposed that nothing, not even the trial, could make one's attitude more positive. Or it may mean that, while there was room for improvement, the trial did not make a contribution in this direction. Clearly, to separate out the two, it would be necessary to have a measurement of sympathy both before and after the trial proceedings. In the absence of such comparative data, results must be interpreted with caution. Yet, as will be shown, there are grounds for believing that the reason the majority of people who reported no improvement did so was not because no room for improvement existed.

It is already evident that the success of the trial was limited. Not everyone paid attention to it and, even among those who did, some failed to learn and to internalize the essential facts of the Nazi atrocities. Criticism of the means that Israel used was associated with rejection of the official estimate as inflated and, in the end, only a minority were moved by the trial to feel greater sympathy for the Jews. But who are the people who felt greater sympathy, and how did they come to feel this way? Of particular significance is whether, in determining sympathy, response to Israel's means took precedence over or was subordinate to understanding the extent of the Nazi atrocities. Only if understanding proved overriding can there be assurance that the trial had even limited success. If people were moved to greater sympathy primarily because they were uncritical of the means, this would be tantamount to the conclusion that they failed to see the basic purpose of the trial or to appreciate its central message.

The evidence is not all in one direction. Sympathy for the Jews was influenced both by response to the means and by whether or not the official version of the Nazi atrocities was accepted. The relative impact of the two forces differed according to how sophisticated the person was as measured by his level of privilege and according to whether or not his acceptance of the official estimate was on the basis of accurate knowledge of it.

Because sophistication was highly related to taking a skeptical attitude toward the trial, one would expect it to be systematically associated with absence of greater sympathy for the Jews. The results bear out this expectation. According to Table 44, each increase in level of sophistication is accompanied by a decrease—especially sharp at the highest levels of sophistication—in the proportion who said they felt more sympathetic toward the Jews as a result of the Eichmann trial.

Knowledge, like sophistication, was also related to being critical of the trial. Again one would expect knowledge to be associated with an absence of greater sympathy for the Jews. The results do not bear out this expectation. Of the poorly informed, 38 per cent, and of the better informed, 36 per cent, expressed greater sympathy for the Jews as a result of the trial.

The absence of a relation between knowledgeability and sympathy is explained by the fact that sympathy is a function not of how much but of what kind of knowledge a person has. Knowledge of Eichmann's capture by Israel in Argentina negatively influenced sympathy. Forty per cent of those who had incomplete knowledge of the capture said that they felt

TABLE 44. TRIAL'S EFFECT ON SYMPATHY TOWARD JEWS BY LEVEL OF SOPHISTICATION
(white respondents only)

Reply to: "*Has the Trial Made You Feel More Sympathetic or Less Sympathetic Toward the Jews?*"	*Level of Sophistication*					
	Low 0	1	2	3	4	*High* 5
More	50%	47%	44%	42%	35%	17%
Less	0	4	2	0	2	3
Same	50	49	54	58	63	80
Number with an opinion	(10)	(51)	(55)	(52)	(63)	(30)
Don't know	17%	7%	5%	2%	2%	3%
Total number	(12)	(55)	(58)	(53)	(64)	(31)

greater sympathy toward the Jews, while 32 per cent of those with complete knowledge said this. On the other hand, knowledge of the official estimate of the number of Jews killed has a positive influence on sympathy: 41 per cent of those who were correctly informed of the official estimate showed greater sympathy as compared to 35 per cent of the misinformed and 33 per cent of the uninformed. While the effect is not strong, it suggests that it was of some importance to the trial's larger goals to communicate the fact of the official estimate to the public.

Since the less sophisticated were relatively uncritical of the trial, it can be conjectured that being uncritical was associated with greater sympathy. Similarly, since those who knew the official estimate tended to accept it more than others, it can be conjectured that acceptance of the estimate was also associated with greater sympathy. Both expectations are confirmed by the data.

Response to the trial's means affected sympathy in the expected direction (Table 45). The more one's image of Eichmann's role conformed to that presented by the prosecution, the more one was inclined to express greater sympathy for the Jews. Similarly, if one thought the trial was legal, one was far more inclined to express greater sympathy than if one thought the trial was not legal.

These observations omit those who were imageless and those who had no opinion on the trial's legality. A singular characteristic of these people, as a second glance at Table 45 will reveal, is that they exhibit little proclivity to express greater sympathy; they most closely resemble the trial's severest critics. The response of the "don't knows" lends support to the view that the question on sympathy is a valid measure of the influence of the trial. If one has not paid enough attention to the trial to form an opinion on some of the main issues it raised, the trial ought not to have had any effect on one's feelings of sympathy.

Responses to Eichmann's complicity and guilt and to the trial's legality each separately had an influence on the amount of sympathy toward the Jewish people generated by the trial. Is the effect also cumulative? To find out, respondents were divided into four groups: those who both accepted the prosecution's depiction of Eichmann as a personal murderer and also saw the trial as legal, those who were accepting on one but not on both of these two issues, those who were negative on both, and those who had no opinion on either question. Respondents were thus divided into those who were uncritical, those who were moderately critical, those who were severely critical, and the "don't knows." When responses to the means are viewed in this way, the results show a clearly cumulative effect: The less the criticism, the greater the sympathy (Table 46). Those without an opinion again most closely resemble the severely critical.

How one felt about Israel's handling of the trial does not

TABLE 47. TRIAL'S EFFECT ON SYMPATHY TOWARD JEWS BY KNOWLEDGE OF OFFICIAL ESTIMATE, SOPHISTICATION, ACCEPTANCE OF OFFICIAL ESTIMATE, AND CRITICISM OF TRIAL MEANS
(white respondents only)

		Per Cent Reporting Greater Sympathy					
Knowledge of Official Estimate	*Sophistication*[a]	Accept Official Estimate	Reject Official Estimate	Percentage Point Difference	Uncritical of means[b]	Critical of means[b]	Percentage Point Difference
Knew	High	44%	(0)	44	42%	45%	—3
Number		(27)	(5)		(24)	(11)	
Knew	Low	52%	42%	10	66%	10%	56
Number		(31)	(12)		(35)	(10)	
Did not know	High	29%	37%	—8	36%	6%	30
Number		(17)	(19)		(25)	(16)	
Did not know	Low	43%	42%	1	49%	27%	22
Number		(44)	(40)		(67)	(11)	

[a] High sophistication is defined as having a score of 4 or 5 on the privilege index; low sophistication, as having a score of 3 or less.

[b] Because the moderately critical resembled the uncritical in their sympathy, they are combined here with the uncritical. The critical comprise only the severely critical.

predict sympathy in an absolute way. However, the two tend to go together. Certainly only a small proportion of those who were severely critical were able to transcend their criticisms

TABLE 46. TRIAL'S EFFECT ON SYMPATHY TOWARD JEWS BY CRITICISM OF TRIAL MEANS
(white respondents only)

	Criticism of Means			
Sympathy Toward Jews	Severely Critical	Moderately Critical	Uncritical	Don't Know
More	21%	45%	59%	27%
Less	2	4	0	0
Same	77	51	41	73
Number with an opinion	(48)	(112)	(41)	(63)
Don't know	4%	1%	5%	10%
Total number	(50)	(113)	(43)	(70)

of the trial and feel greater sympathy for the Jewish people, notwithstanding Israel's hope that this would be the case.

Whether or not people accepted the official version of the Nazi atrocities is less strongly related to sympathy than is response to the means. Insofar as there is a relation, however, it is in the expected direction. Of those who accepted the official estimate, 41 per cent were more sympathetic. The comparable figure for rejecters is 36 per cent and for the "don't knows" 30 per cent.

It is now possible to turn to the question of the relative impact of criticism of the trial and acceptance of the official estimate on sympathy for the Jews. As was indicated earlier, degree of sophistication was one important determinant of the relative weight given to each of the two factors. But whether or not one knew the official estimate beforehand was also of crucial importance.

In order to show the relative impact of acceptance of the official estimate and degree of criticalness, respondents were divided into four groups, depending on their degree of sophistication and on whether they knew the official estimate beforehand. The first row in Table 47 considers the first group: the more sophisticated who knew the official estimate. Among this group, whether one accepted or rejected the official estimate seems to have had a considerable effect on sympathy. Among those who accepted the official estimate, 44 per cent reported greater sympathy. Of the five respondents in this group who rejected the official estimate, not one reported greater sympathy. Degree of criticism had, on the other hand, no significant effect: 42 per cent of the uncritical and 45 per cent of the critical were more sympathetic.

The second row of Table 47 considers the less sophisticated respondents who also knew the official estimate. Whether one accepted or rejected the official estimate made relatively little difference here; accepters and rejecters are separated by only 10 percentage points as far as sympathy is concerned. Criticism of the trial was extremely important: 56 percentage points separate the scores of the critical and noncritical.

Thus, among those who knew the official estimate, whether they accepted it or not made more difference, for the highly sophisticated, than degree of criticism. For the less sophisticated, the opposite was true: Degree of criticism was much more important than acceptance or rejection. Among those who did not know the official estimate (third and fourth rows in Table 47), degree of criticism was more important than acceptance irrespective of sophistication.

These results are based on such a small number of cases that their validity is, to say the least, open to doubt. The findings are internally consistent, however, and they suggest a meaningful interpretation of the process through which the trial generated, or failed to generate, greater sympathy for the Jewish people.

There was always a danger in the Eichmann trial that

TABLE 45. TRIAL'S EFFECT ON SYMPATHY TOWARD JEWS BY IMAGE OF EICHMANN'S COMPLICITY AND GUILT AND BY VIEWS OF THE TRIAL'S LEGALITY
(white respondents only)

	Eichmann's Complicity and Guilt					
Sympathy Toward Jews	Monster (guilty)	Zealot (guilty)	Guilty Bureaucrat	Guiltless Bureaucrat	Imageless Guilty	Imageless, No opinion
More	58%	46%	33%	14%	20%	21%
Less	0	4	0	0	0	0
Same	42	50	67	86	80	79
Number with an opinion	(48)	(81)	(39)	(7)	(30)	(14)
Don't know	4%	1%	0%	0%	9%	18%
Total number	(50)	(82)	(39)	(7)	(33)	(17)

	Legality				
Sympathy Toward Jews	Definitely Legal	Qualified Legal	Qualified Illegal	Definitely Illegal	Don't Know
More	49%	42%	34%	24%	28%
Less	1	2	0	7	0
Same	50	56	66	69	72
Number with an opinion	(96)	(54)	(32)	(42)	(40)
Don't know	2%	5%	0%	5%	11%
Total number	(98)	(57)	(32)	(44)	(45)

people would concentrate whatever attention they gave to it on the way it was handled, and in the process fail to perceive and identify with its more ultimate aims. Judging from the evidence just presented, this was the path most people tended to follow. The manifest purpose of the trial, which was to bring a criminal to justice, dominated their perception of it, and their feelings of sympathy were primarily influenced by whether or not they took a critical stance toward the trial.

The alternative path was to recognize the central issues of the trial and to have one's sympathy determined by one's reaction to the atrocities brought out at the trial. This latter path required a considerable amount of knowledge and sophistication. It required knowledge of the atrocities, whether this knowledge was gained before the trial or during it, and it also required the sophistication to subordinate short-range criticism of the trial to the more ultimate aims it was designed to achieve. It is significant that precisely the sophisticated and knowledgeable segment of the public tended to take this path. The majority lacked either the knowledge or the sophistication, and they tended to lose sight of (if, indeed, they ever understood) the basic purpose of the trial.

The forgoing analysis, besides being based on too few cases, does not wholly explain the factors that won or lost people to greater sympathy. Among the sophisticated and informed, not all accepters of the official estimate exhibited greater sympathy, though it is true that the five rejecters all failed to show greater sympathy. Similarly, criticism or lack of criticism of the means does not wholly account for the variation in sympathy shown by the other three groups. Undeniably this is partly a result of the weakness of the question itself, which does not discriminate the already sympathetic from the nonsympathetic. Moreover, factors other than those chosen for investigation undoubtedly influenced sympathy, though the number of cases precludes carrying the analysis much beyond the point it has reached.

In the interest of understanding the role that anti-Semitism played in forming peoples' responses to the trial, an effort was made to see what effect, if any, anti-Semitism may have had on sympathy. It is useful to be reminded of what has already been learned about the bearing of anti-Semitism on responses to the trial. One of the main effects discovered is that people with anti-Semitic propensities were less inclined to pay attention to and to be informed about the trial than those without such tendencies. Nevertheless, anti-Semitism was found to have no consistent relation to the way people responded to the trial issues once they considered them. Views on Eichmann's complicity and guilt, the trial's legality, and Eichmann's punishment were based on considerations other than respondents' underlying feeling about Jews. This is confirmed once again when, on the basis of their image of Eichmann and their views of the legality of the trial, respondents are separated into critics and noncritics of the trial's means. As Table 48 shows, the proportion scoring anti-Semitic on any of the

TABLE 48. ANTI-SEMITISM AND CRITICISM OF TRIAL MEANS
(white respondents only)

	Acceptance of Means			
Per Cent Anti-Semitic	Severely Critical	Moderately Critical	Uncritical	Don't Know
General index	38%	40%	38%	43%
Number	(45)	(106)	(40)	(56)
Discrimination index	20%	16%	21%	21%
Number	(50)	(113)	(43)	(70)
Self-segregation index	50%	49%	53%	50%
Number	(45)	(102)	(41)	(65)

three measures of anti-Semitism does not vary with degree of criticalness toward the trial.

While unrelated to criticalness, anti-Semitism seemed to reduce acceptance of the official version of the Nazi atrocities, particularly among those who were not correctly informed of it beforehand. Rejecters among both the knowledgeable and the unknowledgeable were more prone to be anti-Semitic than accepters.

With regard to sympathy, the evidence reveals either a small or an inconsistent anti-Semitic effect. Using the general anti-Semitism index, 37 per cent of the anti-Semitic and 41 per cent of the nonanti-Semitic show greater sympathy. Among those who would countenance discrimination against Jews the difference is equally insignificant: 41 per cent and 38 per cent, respectively. There is a moderate effect when self-segregation is used as an indicator of anti-Semitism. Among those who would accept Jews, 43 per cent show greater sympathy as compared to 32 per cent of those not receptive.

This illustrates one of many attempts to establish the effect of anti-Semitism on responses to the question on sympathy. Further comparisons were made controlling for all the variables earlier found to be related to sympathy: sophistication, criticism of the trial, and knowledge and acceptance of the Nazi atrocities. The result was so highly inconsistent as to warrant no other conclusion than that anti-Semitism was not at work in any uniform or systematic way.

It is conceivable that the absence of a consistent effect is the result of inadequacies in the measures of anti-Semitism used. The power of other variables to discriminate anti-Semites from nonanti-Semites, as reported in Appendix B, makes this possibility unlikely. It is also possible that the sympathy measure is inadequate for the purposes for which it has been used. But the power of sophistication, of knowledge and acceptance of the atrocities, and of criticism of the trial to predict sympathy argues against the second possibility. The alternative explanation is that, just as the individual's more basic feelings about Jews were not engaged in his responses to the way the trial was handled, they were not engaged in his response to the question on sympathy.[10]

It is not clear whether the absence of an anti-Semitic effect is the result of a lack of salience of the trial even to the anti-Semite, or of the mildness of present-day anti-Semitic feelings. It would be reassuring to be able to draw the latter conclusion, to be able to assert that anti-Semitism has no serious consequences even when it is confronted by a live issue that affords an opportunity for it to be manifested. However, it is difficult to feel sanguine that this conclusion is correct when so large a proportion of the population examined is willing to express anti-Semitism at an attitudinal level.

THE NEGRO RESPONSE

The response of the Negro community in Oakland to the Eichmann trial was in certain respects strikingly different from that of the white community. Negro respondents were less likely to be aware of the trial than the whites and, once aware, less likely to become highly informed about it. An apparent or surface similarity in Negro and white reactions to the handling of the trial existed, but this turned out to mask rather sharp differences between the two groups. Most notable was the propensity of the more sophisticated Negroes to be uncritical and of the less sophisticated Negroes to be critical of the handling of the trial. In this respect, the relation between being sophisticated and being critical was exactly the

[10] Crespi's conclusions based on the Gallup poll question regarding sympathy for Jews and Israel are similar to ours: ". . . the net favorable reaction to Jews is almost as great among those who said that Jews in this country have too much power as among those who said they have too little. . . . If he sees it as merely another 'human interest' news item, the mildly anti-Semitic person can react with sympathy to the victims of Nazi atrocities without experiencing any conscious conflict of attitudes" (*ibid.*, p. 102).

opposite in the Negro community from what it was in the white community.

With regard to responses to the goals of the trial, a surface similarity is again evident. The proportion who thought that the trial was a good thing was substantially the same in both groups: 83 per cent among the Negroes and 77 per cent among the whites. While whites were more likely than Negroes to know the official estimate (36 per cent versus 23 per cent), there was a high degree of concordance in the proportion of the two groups that accepted the estimate within knowledge categories. Of the knowledgeable Negroes 61 per cent accepted the official estimate as compared to 54 per cent of the whites. Among the uninformed, the difference in the acceptance rate was even less: 32 per cent of the uninformed Negroes and 29 per cent of the uninformed whites accepted the estimate. The similarity also extends to feeling greater sympathy for the Jewish people and for Israel as a result of the trial. Of the Negroes, 40 per cent expressed greater sympathy for the Jews, 35 per cent for Israel. The equivalent figures for whites are 37 per cent and 34 per cent.[11]

These parallels in the responses of the two groups are, of course, incongruous. Given the obvious differences between Negroes and whites in education and socio-economic status, as well as in their general knowledge of the trial, such a high degree of concordance is hardly to be expected. The explanation is, of course, that whites and Negroes of comparable status and knowledge followed quite different courses in deciding their answers to the questions on over-all effect, and the similarity in the results is a statistical artifact.

The analysis of the data has not made fully comprehensible the ways in which white respondents arrived at their net

[11] On the question combining sympathy for Israel and the Jewish people, the Gallup poll results for Negroes are as follows: 30 per cent reported "more sympathy"; 4 per cent, "less sympathy"; 27 per cent, "no difference"; and 39 per cent had no opinion (*ibid.*, p. 95).

reactions to the trial. Nevertheless, it has been possible to explain and understand a considerable amount of the variation in the white response to the trial. The varying responses of the white community are in accord, by and large, with what might have been expected on the basis of past research and theory. This is not so for the Negro responses. The much smaller number of Negro cases precludes analyzing Negro responses as extensively as white responses. But, no matter how far the analysis is taken, the results on over-all impact differ from the white responses, and they are inconsistent with Negro responses to other questions.

When sophistication is controlled, it is found that the least sophisticated Negroes, when they had an opinion, were most likely to exhibit greater sympathy for the Jews (8 out of 16), the most privileged the least likely to do so (1 out of 4). There is no difference in sympathy among the intermediate groups where the bulk of the respondents fall. With only 16 cases in the least privileged group and 4 in the most privileged, little reliance can be placed on the results. Nevertheless, while the results roughly parallel the white response, they do not coincide with the earlier finding that the least sophisticated Negro was apt to be critical rather than uncritical of the means.

The results for knowledge are equally enigmatic. Using the general knowledge index, little difference is found in the response of the three lower knowledge groups; about half express greater sympathy for the Jewish people. But among the eight Negroes who knew the answers to at least three of the four knowledge questions only one expressed greater sympathy. Again the results do not coincide with the earlier findings that with increasing knowledge Negroes tended to become more sympathetic on means.

Using knowledge of the Nazi atrocities as a substitute for the general knowledge index only serves to increase the relation between knowledgeability and an absence of greater sympathy. Among the 21 respondents who knew the official estimate, only 5, or 24 per cent, said they felt greater sympathy. Among the 72 who were uninformed or misinformed about the official estimate, 44 per cent exhibited greater sympathy. Thus, in the Negro community, the relation of knowledge of the atrocities to sympathy is quite different from what it was in the white community. Among whites, while the difference was not great, those who had accurate knowledge of the atrocities were more apt to express greater sympathy than those without such knowledge.

On the other hand, acceptance of the official estimate is related to greater sympathy in the Negro community as well as in the white. Among Negroes who did not know the official estimate, 23 accepted it and 49 did not. But among accepters, 61 per cent, and among nonaccepters, 37 per cent, expressed greater sympathy. Among those who did know the official estimate, there were more accepters than nonaccepters—15 as compared to 6. Of the 15 accepters, 4, or 27 per cent, were more sympathetic; of the 6 nonaccepters, only 1 exhibited greater sympathy. It is clear that when knowledge of the official estimate is held constant, accepters are more apt to be sympathetic than nonaccepters.

As among the whites, sympathy increases as acceptance of the means increases. Only 12 per cent of the highly critical were more sympathetic, as compared with 59 and 53 per cent of the uncritical and the moderately critical. Among those with no opinion on means, 22 per cent scored as more sympathetic.

The bulk of the Negroes (77 per cent) did not know the official estimate. Among this relatively large group, identification with the means and acceptance of the official estimate combined to produce greater sympathy. Of the 17 people who were uncritical on means and also accepted the official estimate, 12, or 71 per cent, express greater sympathy. Twenty-three Negroes were either critical or nonaccepting, and of these 46 per cent were more sympathetic. Of the 5 who were both highly critical and nonaccepting, only 1 showed greater sympathy. The paucity of cases does not permit an assessment of the relative contribution of acceptance of the means and acceptance of the estimate on sympathy among Negroes.

As to the role of anti-Semitism, it apparently did not occur to the Negro anymore than it did to the white that this was a matter to be considered in forming his judgments. There is no evident anti-Semitic effect. Again it is not clear whether this is a result of the lack of salience of the trial to the Negro or the lack of salience of anti-Semitism itself.

This discussion of Negro response to the trial's broader objectives raises more questions than it answers. It has served the important function, however, of suggesting that, even when they share similar or apparently similar socio-economic statuses in society, the Negro views events from a perspective different from that of the white. The fact that the Negro perspective is largely inexplicable is a sign that the social sciences have so far neglected meaningful research on the Negro community. The analysis reported here, though limited and highly tentative, indicates that there is much to be learned about public-opinion formation in this important sector of the polity.

Summary and Conclusions

Three questions were used to measure the over-all impact of the trial. To what extent did the public view the trial as a good thing? To what extent did it both know and accept the official estimate of the number of Jews killed? To what extent did the public feel greater sympathy for the Jewish people as a consequence of the trial? The major aim in analyzing these questions was to discover the extent to which misgivings concerning the conduct of the trial and feelings of prejudice blocked perception and acceptance of its message.

That the trial was generally approved, and that considerable numbers of people were able to transcend their criticism of its details, is evidenced by the fact that 77 per cent of the white awares agreed that the trial was a good thing. Nevertheless, being critical of the details of the trial did dispose people to be critical in their final over-all evaluation. Because sophistication and knowledge led to being critical, and being critical led in turn to withholding over-all approval, it is not surprising to discover that dissatisfaction with the trial, though infrequent in all groups, was greatest among the most sophisticated. Anti-Semitism seemed to play no role in determining respondents' over-all evaluations of the trial.

With regard to knowledge and acceptance of the official estimate, the results support less optimistic conclusions. Only 36 per cent of the white awares had accurate knowledge of the official estimate, and only 54 per cent of these accepted it. Altogether, those who both knew and accepted the official estimate constituted 20 per cent of the white awares. For the first time, anti-Semitism seemed to play a significant role in the responses, being consistently related to rejection among the informed and uninformed alike.

The official estimate was evidently the only issue that tapped the ideology of anti-Semitism. Apparently, the person with anti-Semitic tendencies did not perceive any connection between his feelings toward Jews and the central issues of the trial. He did not judge the trial's legality, and even the question of Eichmann's complicity and guilt, in light of his attitudes toward Jews. Had the anti-Semitic press reached Oaklanders who had ambivalent feelings toward Jews, it is possible that their responses would have been quite different. Lacking such a clue, the anti-Semitically inclined evaluated the trial independently of their negative feelings toward Jews. However, the issue of accepting the official estimate differed from the other issues in one important respect. Rejection of the official estimate is a part of anti-Semitic ideology and was promulgated long before the trial began. Thus, this issue could activate latent anti-Semitism where the other issues could not.

Without a standard of comparison, it is difficult to assess the relative success or failure of the trial in conveying the magnitude of the Nazi atrocities. It is impossible to say whether more Oaklanders knew the official estimate after the trial than before it. It is also impossible to say what proportion of the American public customarily remembers figures it has read in the newspaper. In view of the small extent to which the public has exhibited knowledge of important, heavily reported events in the past, the fact that as many as a third knew the official estimate may be a significant accomplishment. No such sanguine interpretation can be placed, however, on the rate of acceptance among Oaklanders, especially in view of the apparent tendency of anti-Semitic respondents to reject the official estimate.

While knowledge and acceptance of the official estimate were perhaps disappointingly infrequent, they were nevertheless crucial in increasing sympathy for the Jews in the more sophisticated segments of the population. If the respondent was sophisticated enough, and if he comprehended the enormity of the charges against the Nazis, he was able to understand that the central issue of the trial revolved around the historic sufferings of the Jews and not around the proceedings in Jerusalem. If he believed the truth of the charges, he was won to greater sympathy. If he did not believe the charges and rejected the official estimate, he was not won to greater sympathy. In either case, how critical he was of the trial was irrelevant.

The unsophisticated and those who did not fully grasp the

enormity of the charges were not equipped to comprehend the broader implications of the trial. For them, whether or not they accepted the official estimate was a far less important factor than whether or not they were critical of the trial. Among those who merely guessed at the official estimate, acceptance and rejection could not in any case have played a large role; the evidence suggests that in many cases neither acceptance nor rejection was based on conviction. Over and beyond such considerations, however, a profounder conclusion is indicated. This is the conclusion that, while the unsophisticated and unknowledgeable were on the whole uncritical of the trial, when they were critical they were not moved to greater sympathy.

Once again, the Negro response is puzzling. The least sophisticated and least knowledgeable Negroes were most apt to express greater sympathy even though, as earlier analysis showed, they were most apt to be critical of the trial. In sharp contrast to the whites, knowledge of the official estimate did not lead to greater sympathy. However, acceptance of the official estimate did, just as among whites. The paucity of cases made it impossible to carry analysis very far and to assess the extent to which the Negro community was influenced by their criticisms of the trial rather than by acceptance of the official estimate.

CHAPTER 7

CONCLUSIONS AND IMPLICATIONS

YESTERDAY'S events, it has been said, are today's headlines and tomorrow's obituaries. If this is the rule, the Eichmann trial is in part an exception to it. Since Eichmann was executed on May 30, 1962, the trial has continued to be a subject of debate. Stimulated by the publication of Hannah Arendt's controversial interpretation of Eichmann and the role of Jewish leadership in the atrocities,[1] old issues about the trial have been kept alive and new ones introduced.

Despite the spate of continued discussion, there is little doubt that the trial has been as good as forgotten by most of the public. It will not be too long before it is also forgotten by the *avant garde* whose internal dissensions have managed so far to keep it alive. There will be occasions to comment on the trial again as it becomes relevant to future events. But in the end, as with all events, the trial will pass into history.

Unlike the trial itself, the central concern of the trial is not destined to die so quickly. Even as the headlines about the trial disappeared, they were replaced by others underscoring the baffling persistence of anti-Semitism. Whether or not the Eichmann trial won a battle is questionable; that it did not win the war is certain. Anti-Semitism has not yet disappeared from Western society.

[1] Hannah Arendt, *Eichmann in Jerusalem* (New York: Viking Press, 1963). See also Gideon Hausner, *Justice in Jerusalem* (New York: Harper & Row, 1966).

What has been learned about the impact of the Eichmann trial hardly provides a complete strategy for eliminating anti-Semitism. Still, knowledge and understanding about public opinion and public opinion processes can help to inform that effort. To this end, it has seemed useful in this final chapter to review the evidence from this broader perspective.

The first step in any effort to eliminate prejudice is to win the attention of one's intended audience. This is easiest when the audience is a captive one and cannot escape exposure. Even here, of course, the audience has the option of closing its eyes and ears, or of misinterpreting what is going on before it. The Eichmann trial had no captive audience, except for those in the courtroom. If it was to reach the general public, the only channels available to it were the mass media. A spectacular achievement of the trial was the amount and quality of attention it received from the mass media. Over its entire course, the trial was reported on in great detail, for the most part in highly sympathetic terms. If the coverage given to the trial by the mass media is any criterion, the public had more than ample opportunity to become exposed to the trial and its message.

Despite the opportunity, few people took advantage of it. The trial was not able to transcend the general tendency of people to ignore the serious news event. To be sure, only 16 per cent of the sample missed it entirely. At the same time, only 13 per cent paid enough attention to it to be able to answer correctly four elementary questions on the details of the trial and its background. Even these people did not single out the trial for special attention; they customarily pay attention to *all* serious news events.

Involving people in the trial could not have guaranteed the achievement of its educational objectives. Involvement in an issue may produce a boomerang effect instead of the intended one. Nevertheless, a prerequisite for conveying the message of the trial was that the public be persuaded to pay attention to it. Judged on this criterion alone, the trial failed in large measure to achieve its purpose.

The question may be raised as to whether the apathy exhibited by the public was inevitable. As the Negroes' responses to the Freedom Riders indicates, greater involvement would have been achieved had it been possible to make the trial personally relevant to more people. It is difficult, however, to imagine anything that Israel could have done to imbue the trial with this kind of salience. Much of the public was apathetic when the Nazi persecutions were taking place. To overcome this apathy some twenty years later by reminding people of what they had allowed to happen was a remote possibility indeed.

The trial, while failing to win everybody's interest, did engage the attention of that small proportion of the public most disposed to become involved in public affairs. These are people who not only have the greatest stake in the larger society but also have the greatest opportunity to inform the larger society. Presuming no boomerang effect, it would have been preferable had the trial reached everybody with its message. As a second choice, however, it would seem that the trial could have done no better than to reach the group most likely in the long run to inform the society's general values.

This somewhat optimistic interpretation is tempered by the earlier observation that those who gave most attention to the trial were the kind of people apt to give attention to any serious news event. There is no indication that the trial was singled out for special attention. More than this, there are grounds for asserting that, since they are the least likely to harbor anti-Semitic beliefs, the "elite" were not the most important segment of the audience to reach. Presuming once again a persuasive power of a positive kind, the trial could potentially have made a more significant impact had it elicited greater attention from those with the strongest proclivities toward anti-Semitism. This, the evidence has shown, it did not do. While some anti-Semites paid attention, the general tendency was for them to avoid exposure to the trial.

Whether the standard is imposed that the trial's goals were realizable only if everybody paid attention or, alternatively, that it would have been a satisfactory achievement so long as those most needful of the message paid attention, the trial failed on both counts. However, bearing in mind the differential response of the informed and the uninformed, there is reason to believe that more widespread involvement in the trial would have been self-defeating. Before pursuing this possibility, it is necessary to summarize what that response was.

The failure of the trial to overcome public complacence, while virtually assuring the failure of its ultimate educational objectives, did not eliminate all possibility of a positive effect. There was nothing to be hoped for, of course, from the minority who were not even aware that the trial was going on. The prospect remained, however, that in spite of their relative apathy, the majority who paid only scant attention to the trial would come away from it feeling more positive toward Israel and more sympathetic to the Jewish people. Moreover, there was the larger prospect that the small but elite group who did pay attention would be deeply moved and persuaded of the need to eradicate anti-Semitism.

To a surprising extent, the trial did win the sympathy of the apathetic majority. Most of them felt that the trial was a good thing, and many were moved to feel greater sympathy for Israel and the Jewish people. Moreover, they were relatively uncritical of those actions on which sophisticated observers thought Israel was most vulnerable.

Is this generally uncritical and sympathetic response to be

taken seriously? Or does it merely mean that the apathetic majority tends to adopt the prevailing attitude of the mass media? These people were not really involved in the drama of the trial. They were likely not to know who Eichmann was, and not to have grasped the enormity of the Nazi atrocities. Their favorable response appeared to be largely a reflection of their desire to conform to the favorable attitudes they discerned in the mass media. Had the mass media adopted a negative stance, the apathetic majority might well have responded in kind.

While there is obvious validity in such observations, they overlook the fact that people rarely take the trouble to inform themselves about the details of current issues. Nevertheless, most of them form opinions even when they know very little. These opinions may not be profound, but they do establish the framework within which people think and, when the occasion arises, act. Uninformed opinions cannot be discarded as irrelevant.

It is in the trial's favor, therefore, that it succeeded in generating a friendly and sympathetic response among the apathetic majority. It could not hope radically to alter present anti-Semitic beliefs and attitudes. Nevertheless, any reinforcement of friendly feelings toward Jews, if it can be sustained, is likely to be cumulative and, in the long run, to whittle away at the persistent residue of anti-Semitism.

That the mass media were the instruments through which this generally positive response was elicited is also of importance since there is widespread agreement among communications researchers that the mass media are seldom the dominant influence in opinion formation.[2] Mass media may reinforce pre-existing tendencies toward a particular viewpoint or establish the issues on which opinions are to be

[2] Joseph T. Klapper, *The Effects of Mass Communication,* (Glencoe, Ill.: The Free Press, 1960).

formed, but it has been confirmed that people act out of some combination of self-interest and personal values, and will not automatically follow the advice of the mass media.

However, most communications research has focused on issues of high salience, such as voting for high public office. Moreover, the effects studied have been short-term rather than long-term ones. By concentrating on highly salient issues and by ignoring long-run effects research has overlooked a possibly powerful cumulative mass media effect on issues which remain of low salience for extended periods of time. On such issues, the majority do not take the trouble to become even minimally informed so that they can arrive at an independent judgment. Rather, when it becomes appropriate for them to have an opinion, they search for clues as to what proper opinion is. A natural source is the impressions they have been absorbing almost subliminally from habitual, if superficial, attention to the mass media. This would appear to be the process through which the apathetic majority formed their generally favorable opinion about the trial. They were primed to form this opinion not only by what they discerned to be the proper attitude from their limited exposure to the trial via the mass media, but by prior exposure to what may be described as a long-term propensity on the part of the mass media to present stories about Jews in a sympathetic light.

If it is generally true that the mass media have a large role in determining the climate of mass opinion on issues of low salience, then over the long run they must help to establish the perspective from which issues are evaluated when they do in fact become salient. By itself, a stimulus such as the Eichmann trial is not likely to have much effect. However, seen as one of a series of stimuli directed to establishing a sympathetic image of the Jewish people, it is of some importance that the trial did make a positive impression on most people, even though the impression lacked depth because at the time the underlying issue of anti-Semitism lacked salience.

There is always the danger that the mass media may not be persuaded to present an issue from a particular point of view. Here Israel took a calculated risk, and her success in winning the mass media to her side paid off in the positive response she obtained from a majority of the public.

These observations pertain to the apathetic majority. What about the elite few who, while not deeply involved, nevertheless knew what the issue was all about? Their judgments are likely to count for more than those of the apathetic majority in informing public values. In the case of the Eichmann trial, the burden of Israel's case rested on the assumption that once people understood what the Nazis had done, they could not fail to be persuaded to her cause. The intervening factor which partially upset this expectation was Israel's handling of the trial. A persistent finding of the study is that those who knew the most about the trial and who, in addition, could evaluate what they knew in a sophisticated way, were the most disposed to be critical of Israel's means. Knowledge and sophistication, instead of winning acceptance of Israel's actions, encouraged rejection.

Criticism was tempered in some cases by an appreciation of the purposes of the trial. In line with Israel's expectations, this happened most notably when there was understanding of the extent of the Nazi atrocities. Unfortunately, most of the informed critics were not so discerning. They were unable to transcend their rejection of Israel's means to the extent of feeling greater sympathy for the Jewish people. But among the informed a sophisticated few were able to feel sympathy for the ends despite their reservations about the means.

The results suggest that these sympathetic critics were persuaded beforehand of the correctness of Israel's cause, but the trial made them uneasy because they were unsure about Israel's means. While personally able to tolerate the ambiguity in these means, they sensed that this may not have been true of everybody. Running through their responses was an anxiety, akin to that expressed in the sophisticated media, that Israel was damaging her own interests by the way she handled the trial. By and large the anxiety proved to be unjustified. The masses did not perceive the ambiguity of the means; if a boomerang response occurred, it was minimal.

The prevailing values of a democracy are not contributed to equally by all of its citizens. What the enlightened few think, feel, and say counts heavily in establishing the standards against which the society measures its performance. The Eichmann trial probably did very little to reinforce the commitment of the enlightened to a cause they had internalized ahead of time. In fact, it created uneasiness among a substantial number of them. Nevertheless, the trial demonstrated that the commitment existed and that it was often strong enough to withstand the misgivings prompted by Israel's actions.

Viewed as a whole, the results suggest that Israel achieved all that she could reasonably have expected from the trial, given the nature of public opinion and public-opinion processes. Indeed, had she succeeded in transcending such processes and imbued the trial with enough salience to involve everybody, the chances are that the net effect would have damaged rather than advanced her cause. Generating greater involvement in the trial would have been to Israel's interest only if involvement would have produced acceptance of the way that she handled the trial or recognition of and sympathy for her larger purposes in conducting the trial. Very few, to be sure, were deeply involved in the trial. Nevertheless, there was considerable variation in interest. The more interest people manifested, as indicated by their level of knowledge, the more critical they were on means. It can be assumed, therefore, that had a larger proportion of the population shown interest, the effect would have been to produce greater criticism than was actually exhibited. With deeper interest, the ambiguities of Israel's handling of the trial would simply have become more visible.

Even this would not necessarily have been prejudicial to the trial had the critics been able to disentangle the means from the ends and then accept the ends despite being critical of the means. The evidence suggests that only the more sophisticated respondents were able to do this. Less sophisticated people who knew what was going on based their final judgments of the trial on their reactions to its means. Since the majority of the uninformed were also unsophisticated, it follows that the effect of involving the unsophisticated more deeply in the trial may well have produced not only greater criticism on means but a larger over-all negative impact as well.

It was apparently not an unfortunate circumstance for Israel that a majority of the public remained apathetic about the trial. It may even be fortunate that the issue of anti-Semitism was not made salient in a context in which the ambiguities inherent in Israel's handling of the trial threatened a boomerang effect. This is not to say that public complacence about the issue of anti-Semitism is generally desirable. Where the general climate is friendly toward Jews and where acts of discrimination are on the wane, the lack of salience of anti-Semitism to the general public may be helpful rather than harmful. However, a complacent public is not likely to be an effectively armed public should organized anti-Semitism ever gain a substantial foothold. The majority of the German public may not have been strongly anti-Semitic when the Nazis first initiated their persecution of the Jews. It is possible that the ability of the Nazis to pursue their evil was a result less of an aroused public than of an apathetic public, ill-motivated and ill-equipped to resist the mobilized and committed minority.

There is some warrant for saying that it could never happen in the United States. American society is not the same as German society. In American ideals of democracy and in the stability of its political institutions, the necessary bulwark to protect America from violent and widespread anti-Semitism would appear to be present. Viewed from one perspective, the evidence from the present study is reassuring in this regard. The residue of anti-Semitism that still exists in the United States was apparently not engaged by the trial. This suggests that anti-Semitism may not be strong enough to trigger action even when this involves no more than expressing critical opinions of the Eichmann trial.

One cannot be sure, however. The possibility exists that the lack of engagement was simply a result of the trial's lack of salience. That there is a sizable residue of anti-Semitic feeling, and that those with such proclivities were prone to avoid exposure to the trial and to reject the official estimate of the Nazi crimes against Jews, offsets to some extent other evidence that anti-Semitism was not a significant factor in influencing opinions about the trial itself.

Public complacence will no longer be an issue for anti-Semitism when no one has anti-Semitic beliefs and feelings or when no one is motivated to act on them. In the interim, however, those who are concerned that it not happen in America can no more ignore public complacence about the issue than they can the persistence of anti-Semitism itself.

Viewed from this broad perspective, the Eichmann trial appears to have been almost redundant. It seems to have made no progress in overcoming public complacence or in routing out the residue of deep-seated anti-Semitic prejudice. Such tasks, however, are not likely to be accomplished by a single stimulus. Arousing moral concern about prejudice and eventually eliminating it will occur only when these tasks are thoroughly integrated into the socialization process. Perhaps the only way to do this is to build on and to reinforce, over an extended period of time, the seemingly superficial but nevertheless positive climate of opinion that now characterizes feelings about Jews. An ever more favorable climate of opinion, no matter how lacking in depth, may be the only avenue for such opinion to enter into the socialization process as a matter of course. In this sense, the Eichmann trial undoubtedly made a positive contribution. The general climate of opinion would appear to be better rather than worse because the trial took place.

The most general point which these observations suggest is that the ability of a democracy to survive virtually requires an apathetic majority on domestic issues. International issues, it should be pointed out, do not follow the same rule. The public may indeed become deeply involved in such issues as they did in the Cuban crisis. However, on international issues, a deeply involved public is not likely to be a divided public. Rather, if an international issue is serious enough to involve everybody, the effect is likely to be a binding together around a common position to oppose the threat from outside. Wholesale involvement of everyone in all domestic issues, however, would generate cleavages that a democracy would not be able to withstand for long. The success of American democracy is based in no small measure on the fact that throughout its history very few issues have deeply involved and divided the total public. The slavery issue in the last century was one exception, and this issue led to the Civil War.

In this regard, the problem of anti-Semitism in America bears comparison with the problem of racial prejudice. The two issues are in some respects strikingly similar and in others radically different. On both issues, the mass media in this country appear to be largely committed to a sympathetic stance. In their treatment of news stories and in their editorial positions, they reflect a concern to create a climate of opinion that will foster the elimination of prejudice, whatever its form. The attitude of the mass media both reflects and is reflected in the attitudes of the sophisticated elite. On the issue of prejudice, the mass media and the sophisticated elite have managed to shape the commitment of the larger society toward the value of tolerance. That there has been a large increase in favorable attitudes toward Negroes since 1945 has been impressively demonstrated for both North and South,[3] and in some respects this change is even more dramatic than the decrease in anti-Semitism during this same period.

Perhaps the crucial difference between the two issues is that the one—racial prejudice—is at the present time highly salient in American society, whereas the other—anti-Semitism—is not. The greater salience of racial prejudice can be attributed to the current struggle for equal rights and the fact that this struggle calls for radical and rapid changes in the *status quo*. It demands not only that traditional values be sacrificed but that people change their way of doing things and even agree to renounce prerogatives and privileges long enjoyed. Moreover, these changes would affect large numbers of people, and affect them in fundamental ways.

It is instructive to note, however, that not all Negro rights are denied with equal force in all parts of the country. In the South, where Negroes are often in the majority and their subservience has long been extreme, even Negro voting rights are denied. In the South, there is no apathetic majority, and the more tolerant attitudes of the elite have had little effect in changing the civil status of Negroes. Firms which in the

[3] Paul B. Sheatsley, "White Attitudes Toward the Negro," *Daedalus*, Winter 1966, pp. 217–238.

North may be willing to hire Negroes for more than menial positions do not do so in the South; to the Southern communities in which they are established, any hint of equality for Negroes is salient and threatening. In the North, on the other hand, where public opinion is largely indifferent to the question of equal job opportunities for Negroes, the more tolerant attitudes of community and government leaders tend to prevail, at least when spurred by Negro protest. Indeed, if anything, the Negro's problem in the North is less that of fighting adamant opposition than of coping with widespread indifference and apathy. The same does not hold for equal housing opportunities; on this issue the majority is far from apathetic, and residential segregation in the North seems destined for a longer life than many other forms of discrimination.

Concerning anti-Semitism, it is difficult to imagine a way in which the elimination of prejudice toward Jews could possibly entail both radical changes in established institutions and value systems and the involvement of large numbers of people in these changes. The possibility of anti-Semitism's becoming a major issue in the United States lies more in a prejudiced elite gaining control over an apathetic majority than in the overturn of a sympathetic government by a prejudiced and involved public.

For those concerned to contain and eventually eliminate anti-Semitism, this suggests the constant need to reinforce the existing sympathies of that section of the elite committed to tolerance. In this respect, the Eichmann trial avoided being self-defeating almost in spite of itself. Had the elite been less sympathetic to begin with, the chances are that their negative response to its means would not have been overcome by a sympathetic reaction to the goals of the trial.

These summary observations about the trial have been based on the results viewed broadly. It is left to the reader to discover the fine points, the specifications, and the exceptions to these observations that can be found in the more detailed report of the findings. However, there is one subsidiary finding that deserves some comment in bringing the book to a close. This is the response of the Negro community to the trial.

There was a basic difference in the source of favorable and unfavorable comment in the white and Negro communities. Among whites, criticism tended to stem from the more sophisticated and privileged part of the population. Among Negroes, it was the least sophisticated and most deprived who were the most critical. The sparseness of Negroes in the sample prevented analysis of this peculiar reversal in the Negro response, and little could be done beyond speculating as to its source. It was surmised that in being critical the more deprived Negro was giving expression to his general alienation from the norms and the justice of white society.

It need hardly be said that such speculation has to be tested by further research. Presuming that it is true, its potential importance lies in what it may imply for a rise in anti-Semitism in the Negro community. Generally speaking, when differences in socio-economic status are taken into account, the Negroes in the sample were, if anything, slightly less anti-Semitic than the whites. Moreover, as with the whites, anti-Semitism did not appear to be a major factor influencing responses to the trial. Nevertheless, there is the possibility that, if the alienation of the deprived Negro is aggravated, his rejection of the prevailing norms will serve to increase his anti-Semitism. This is only speculation; yet the issue raised is serious enough to warrant further investigation and will be treated in a future volume in this series.

APPENDIXES

APPENDIX A

METHODOLOGICAL NOTES

Sample Design and Execution

The primary source of data for this study was a probability sample of persons sixteen years of age or older residing in the cities of Oakland and Piedmont, California. According to the 1960 census, Oakland had a population of 367,548; Piedmont, one of 11,147. Piedmont forms an enclave within Oakland. It is in many respects part of the same community, and was so considered in this study.

A multistage, stratified area sample was used, designed to be approximately self-weighting. The primary sampling units were the 100 census tracts of the two cities. These were divided into three strata by their median monthly rental as reported in the 1960 census. Each stratum was constructed so that it contained almost exactly a third of the population to be studied. Within each stratum, nine census tracts were selected by systematic random sampling with probability proportionate to size. Only 25 tracts, rather than 27, were obtained by this procedure, as two tracts were selected twice.

Enumeration districts were used as the second stage. Two districts were drawn for the two tracts doubly chosen at the first stage, and one district was drawn for each of the remaining tracts. Again, systematic random sampling with probability proportionate to size was employed. A total of 27 enumeration districts resulted.

A team of enumerators was then employed to list all dwelling units in each of the 27 districts. A total of 10,806 dwelling units were found. The 1960 census reported 10,848 units for the same districts. For each district an equal-probability random sample of 22 dwelling units was chosen for interviewing. Units found to be vacant or to have been converted to nonresidential purposes at the time of the field work were replaced by other randomly chosen units.

Within each selected household, an enumeration of all persons over the age of sixteen was made by the interviewer, who then referred to a special table printed on the assignment sheet to select the household member to be interviewed at that address. Eight different sets of tables were used and systematically distributed among the assignment sheets so that the procedure would closely approximate a simple random sampling of the respondents within the household. Thus the interviewer had no control over which adult would be interviewed. In the few cases where the incorrect person was interviewed, the interviewer was sent back to the household to obtain an interview with the correct person.

Because households were selected with equal probability within the districts, a slight bias was introduced through the inclusion of a disproportionate number of persons living in households with less than the average number of adults. For example, persons living in households with no other adults had a probability of 1.00 of being selected at the final stage of sampling, while those living in households with four other adults had a probability of 0.20 of being chosen. The limitations of this method of sampling were recognized from the outset, but this approach was used because previous studies have indicated that the bias introduced is small. In the present study, the extent of bias was examined by weighting the responses of each person by the number of adults in his household. In no case was there a difference of more than three percentage points between the marginals of the weighted and unweighted figures on any of the questionnaire items.

A battery of techniques was employed to complete interviews with as large a proportion of the selected respondents as possible. Calls were made at the housing unit until contact with some member of the household was made and an enumeration taken. At this point either the designated respondent was interviewed or an attempt was made to set up an appointment for a later interview. A person was not counted as a refusal until he had refused three separate interviewers, and a person was not classified as "not at home" until attempts to reach him had failed at least six different times. If the respondent spoke a foreign language, an attempt was made to find someone to interpret, and several interviews were conducted in Spanish. Negro respondents who refused to be interviewed, or who could not be found by white interviewers, were assigned to Negro interviewers, with great success. Respondents who terminated the interview before its completion were recontacted by the same interviewer, or by a different one if the characteristics of the first interviewer were felt to be a possible cause of the break-off. All ill persons were recontacted at a later time. In a very small number of cases, occurring at the end of the field period, it was not possible to apply all of these techniques. With most subjects, however, the minimum number of contacts for refusals, not-at-homes, ill persons, and break-offs were exceeded before they were considered uninterviewable.

The net result of these procedures was that interviews were conducted at 78 per cent of the occupied dwelling units, a total of 463 completed interviews. In California, the problems with not-at-home respondents seem to be much greater than in the East, first because of the climate, and second because of the recreation facilities available. The problem exists during the entire year but is especially acute during the summer when the field work was conducted. The rate of refusals and inaccessibles seems about average for a very tight probability sample such as the one used here. If substitutions had been made after three calls for the not-at-homes and after one for refusals or whenever the subject was found to be ill or out of town, the complete sample of 584 could have been obtained. The use of liberal substitutions, however, would overrepresent those people who are most accessible and thus add an additional bias to the sample. The decision to keep a tight probability sample and accept the losses seemed to represent the most accurate approach available.

Index of Occupational Prestige

1. Low-low, e.g., garbage collector, pin setter, janitor, ordinary seaman, shoe shiner, farm laborer, tenant-farmer.
2. Middle-low, e.g., postman, fireman, policeman, barber, clerk in a retail store, mechanic, bus driver, longshoreman.
3. High-low and low-high, e.g., skilled workers (plumber, carpenter, electrician), owner of small retail or service business (tailor shop, ice cream parlor, television repair, shoe repair, grocer), locomotive engineer, tool and die maker, foreman or white-collar supervisor with minimum discretion and/or small staff, small-farm owner or manager.
4. Middle-high, e.g., superskilled (airline pilot, engineer without professional degree, diamond cutter), primary or secondary school teacher or principal, semiprofessional (mortician, pharmacist, social worker, clergyman without professional degree), wholesale salesman (i.e., salesman to firms), middle manager, dentist, large-farm owner or manager.
5. High-high, e.g., old-line professional (lawyer, physician, college professor, architect), president of medium to large firm, top management of large firm, military above colonel (Army) or captain (Navy), self-supporting highbrow (e.g., writer).
6. Unclassifiable; includes "no answer."

Index of Social Privilege

A general description of the index of social privilege may be found in Chapter 2. It should be added that originally there were 60 cases—34 whites and 26 Negroes—who could not be scored on the privilege index because of missing information. In every case but one, these respondents had failed to report their income or their occupation. The following procedure was used to score these cases on the index of social privilege.

Where either income or occupation was not reported, education was accorded double weight. This procedure allowed 52 cases to be scored on the index. Two Negroes who, on the basis of this procedure, would have advanced into the small category of the highly privileged were not scored because their inclusion into so small a group was risky. Five cases who reported neither income nor occupation were not given scores. Finally, in the single case where there was no information regarding home ownership, the respondent was not advanced on the privilege scale because both his income and his occupation were low.

Analysis revealed that the rescored cases behaved like other individuals on the same level of privilege when variables related to privilege were introduced. In addition, most tables were run using both the original index and the revised index; comparison of these measures showed that no significant differences existed. The advantage of the revised index is that it augments the working sample, and for this reason is used throughout the analysis.

General Anti-Semitism Index

The general anti-Semitism index is based on a factor analysis of twenty-five items in the interview schedule taken from T. W. Adorno *et al., The Authoritarian Personality.*[1] Included (see Appendix C) were questions tapping anti-Semitic feelings, *F* (or so-called authoritarianism), anti-Negro feelings, and ethnocentrism. Owing to the presence of items concerning Negroes, separate factor analyses were done for Negroes and whites. The analysis yielded clear anti-Semitism, *F*, and anti-Negro factors among the whites. The five major items in the white anti-Semitism factor were examined for their intercorrelations among Negroes. The following three were highly intercorrelated in both groups,

1. Anyone who employs many people should be careful not to hire a large percentage of Jews.
2. Jews don't like to mix with other people so they would rather live in special areas of their own.
3. The trouble with letting Jews into a nice neighborhood is that they gradually give it a typically Jewish atmosphere.

[1] New York: Harper & Row, 1950.

Intercorrelations (Q's) between these items for the total sample are:

1	2	3
–	.70	.75
	–	.70

Discrimination Index

The discrimination index was based on the four questions listed below. A responses were counted as discriminatory; B responses, as nondiscriminatory. Although "don't know" was not offered as a response category, on each question some respondents gave this reply or refused to answer.

1. As you may know, many vacation resorts in the United States refuse to accept Jews as guests. Will you please tell me which of these statements comes closest to your own feelings on this matter?

A. Christians have a right to expect that a vacation resort will cater only to other Christians like themselves.

B. Jews have a right to expect that a vacation resort will accept them on the same basis as Christians.

2. How would you feel if one of the biggest companies in town said it was going to set a limit on the number of Jews it has in the better jobs. Which of these statements comes closest to your feelings on this matter?

A. I'd think it was a good idea; Jews get more than their share of the better jobs anyway.

B. Jews should have the same chance to get the better jobs as anyone else.

3. If a candidate for Congress in this state should declare himself as being against the Jews, would this influence you to vote for him, or against him?

A. Vote for him.

B. Vote against him.

4. Would you vote for a Jew for President of the United States if he were well qualified for this position?

A. Yes.
B. No.

Owing to the small number of people who explicitly endorsed discrimination, the following scoring procedure was adopted. To be classified as a nondiscriminator, a person had to give four nondiscriminatory responses. If he gave even one discriminatory response, he was classified as a discriminator. All others were categorized as mixed. Using this procedure, 232 respondents were classified as nondiscriminators, 126 as mixed, and 100 as discriminators; the five Jewish respondents were excluded.

Self-Segregation Index

In the course of the interview, respondents were given the following instructions: "On each of the cards in this stack [stack handed to respondent] is a word or two that are sometimes used to describe different types of people. Please read each of the cards, and then put into one pile the types of people you *yourself* would *like* to have marry into your immediate family, and into the other pile the types of people you would *not like* to have marry into your immediate family."

The cards (see Appendix C, item 27) listed fifty-three groups representing different religions, political orientations, regions, races, educational and class levels, nationalities, and occupations. The cards were shuffled by the interviewer prior to each interview so that possible ordering effects would be randomized.

A self-segregation index was constructed on the basis of responses to the following groups only: English, Irish, German, Italian, Polish, Jewish, Israeli, Mexican, Arab, Japanese, African, and Negro. Responses to the question on marital acceptability were then intercorrelated. These correlations yielded a ranking of ethnic groups in terms of their acceptability: The order is the same as that given above. The joint distribution of these twelve items was then examined, and it became apparent that these twelve items formed a Guttman scale. The scale has a reproducibility of 0.93.

The Guttman scale types received a score equivalent to their rank (see chart below). All Guttman error types were rescored and grouped with the scale type most similar to the original response type.

PATTERNS OF ACCEPTANCE

Would Accept	English	Irish	German	Italian	Pole	Jew	Israeli	Mexican	Arab	Japanese	African	Negro
All	+	+	+	+	+	+	+	+	+	+	+	+
African	+	+	+	+	+	+	+	+	+	+	+	−
Japanese	+	+	+	+	+	+	+	+	+	+	−	−
Arab	+	+	+	+	+	+	+	+	+	−	−	−
Mexican	+	+	+	+	+	+	+	+	−	−	−	−
Israeli	+	+	+	+	+	+	+	−	−	−	−	−
Jew	+	+	+	+	+	+	−	−	−	−	−	−
Pole	+	+	+	+	+	−	−	−	−	−	−	−
Italian	+	+	+	+	−	−	−	−	−	−	−	−
German	+	+	+	−	−	−	−	−	−	−	−	−
Irish *or*	+	+	−	−	−	−	−	−	−	−	−	−
English	+	−	−	−	−	−	−	−	−	−	−	−
No one	−	−	−	−	−	−	−	−	−	−	−	−

In analyzing the data, this scale was dichotomized as indicated above.

APPENDIX B

ANTI-SEMITISM IN OAKLAND

This appendix deals with the social sources of anti-Semitism in the Oakland sample. It has been prepared, in part, in the interest of validating the measures of anti-Semitism used in the study. In addition, the findings are of intrinsic interest for what they reveal about the extent and location of anti-Semitism in a modern American metropolis.

Three measures of anti-Semitism were used in the study. These have been described at some length in Chapter 2 and in Appendix A. Briefly, for the general anti-Semitism index, individuals were scored by the number of anti-Semitic responses to three belief items. The second measure, the index of discrimination, classified individuals by their degree of acceptance of discriminatory practices against Jews. The third measure, the self-segregation index, was designed to tap feelings of social distance from Jews. In effect it separated those who would from those who would not like a Jew to marry into their families.

To simplify presentation, this analysis focuses on the general index of anti-Semitism. This index measures only one component of anti-Semitism—negative beliefs about Jews—but it is systematically related to both discrimination and self-segregation as well as to other indicators of anti-Semitism. This is demonstrated in Table B-1.

For every increase on the general index of anti-Semitism, greater proportions give an anti-Semitic response on both the discrimination and the self-segregation measures. For example, 14 per cent of the group with a score of zero on the general index

TABLE B-1. SCORES ON THE GENERAL INDEX OF ANTI-SEMITISM AND ANTI-SEMITIC RESPONSES TO RELATED INDICATORS

Per Cent Who Gave Anti-Semitic Response to:	*General Index of Anti-Semitism* Low 0	1	2	High 3	*Total*
Discrimination index	14%	27%	40%	56%	22%
Self-segregation index	34	60	69	73	43
Have you entertained a Jew in your home during the past year? No.	57	82	89	96	67
There may be a few exceptions, but in general, Jews are pretty much alike.	56	77	76	81	57
There is some basic Jewish quality that resists the American melting pot and makes Jews different from other people.	18	53	66	72	31
I can hardly imagine myself marrying a Jew.	32	53	69	73	40
One trouble with Jewish businessmen is that they stick together and connive, so that a Gentile doesn't have a fair chance in competition.	23	51	77	81	34
Number	(213)	(92)	(50)	(27)	(458)[a]

[a] The base for the total column is the total number of respondents in the sample. The body of the table, however, excludes 76 cases who could not be scored on the anti-Semitism index because of their failure to answer the relevant questions. Analysis of these cases revealed that their attitudes toward Jews fell between those who scored zero on the index and those who scored 1. Further analysis revealed that no social group is disproportionately represented among the unclassified cases. Consequently, their omission does not seriously bias the results.

were found to be anti-Semitic on the discrimination index, as compared to 27 per cent, 40 per cent, and 56 per cent who had a score of 1, 2, and 3, respectively. This general pattern also applies using the other indicators of anti-Semitism. All in all, the general index of anti-Semitism appears to distinguish effectively between different degrees of anti-Semitism.

The "Total" column on the right of Table B-1 shows the proportion of the sample who gave an anti-Semitic response to each item. Hence, 22 per cent accepted discrimination, 43 per cent were self-segregating, and so on. How much anti-Semitism exists in Oakland depends on how the phenomenon is defined. Whatever the definition, however, it is evident that a substantial minority of the Oakland sample exhibited some proclivity toward anti-Semitism.

What kinds of Oaklanders are most prone to exhibit anti-Semitic tendencies? The answer, generally speaking, is: those people who are economically, socially, and culturally deprived. However the data are examined, this general tendency manifests itself in a remarkably uniform way.

The idea that people differ in economic privilege was developed at some length in Chapter 2. There, level of economic privilege was found to be strongly related to exposure to the trial. The more economically deprived a respondent was, the less was his exposure to the trial. Applying this same idea to the phenomenon of anti-Semitism, level of economic privilege is about as strongly predictive of anti-Semitism as it was of exposure to the trial.

The components of the index of economic privilege, it will be recalled, were education, income, prestige of occupation, and home ownership. Table B-2 shows how each of these components is related to anti-Semitism as measured by the general index. In each case, the deprived elements—the uneducated, the poor, those in low-prestige jobs, and renters—are more likely to be anti-Semitic.[1]

[1] The figures for education would appear on close examination to belie the uniformity of the general tendency. The most disprivileged—those with a grammar school diploma or less—are the most likely to be anti-Semitic (66 per cent), and the most privileged—the postgraduates—the least likely

TABLE B-2. ANTI-SEMITISM BY EDUCATION, INCOME, OCCUPATION, AND HOME OWNERSHIP[a]

Education

	Eighth Grade or Less	Some High School	Finished High School	Business or Trade School	Some College	Finished College	Post-graduate
Per cent anti-Semitic	66%	51%	30%	56%	43%	21%	20%
Number	(85)	(89)	(94)	(16)	(49)	(24)	(25)

Annual Family Income

	Under $2,000	$2,000–$3,999	$4,000–$5,999	$6,000–$7,999	$8,000–$9,999	$10,000–$14,999	Above $15,000
Per cent anti-Semitic	64%	50%	47%	36%	45%	37%	19%
Number	(44)	(66)	(88)	(61)	(44)	(38)	(27)

Occupational Prestige

	Lower	Lower Middle	Middle	Upper Middle	Upper
Per cent anti-Semitic	52%	48%	46%	28%	26%
Number	(58)	(109)	(99)	(65)	(19)

Home Ownership

	Renters	Homeowners
Per cent anti-Semitic	47%	42%
Number	(157)	(224)

[a]Unless otherwise stated, a person is defined as anti-Semitic if he has a score of 1, 2, or 3 on the index of anti-Semitism. Note in Table B-1 that the group with a score of 1 on the index more closely resembles the group scoring 3 than the group that had no anti-Semitic responses. This "natural break" warrants the division of the index into two parts: the nonanti-Semitic who constitute 56 per cent of the sample and the anti-Semitic who constitute the remaining 44 per cent.

When the index of economic privilege is substituted for its components, the result is to show that with each decrease in privilege, the proportion scoring as anti-Semitic increases (Table

TABLE B-3. ANTI-SEMITISM BY INDEX OF ECONOMIC PRIVILEGE

	Index of Economic Privilege				
	Low 0	1	2	3	High 4
Per cent anti-Semitic	64%	50%	41%	36%	26%
Number	(63)	(109)	(86)	(56)	(61)

B-3). Among the most deprived, 64 per cent scored as anti-Semitic. Among the most privileged, 26 per cent did so.

The economically deprived are also likely to be socially deprived. However, social deprivation may exist without economic deprivation. Social deprivation, as it is here conceived, is a derivative of society's propensity to value some attributes of individuals and groups more highly than others and to distribute prestige, power, status, and opportunities accordingly. Social deprivation, then, arises out of the differential distribution of highly regarded social attributes.

The indicators that might be used to distinguish the socially privileged from the socially deprived are virtually endless. In American society, for example, youth is regarded more highly than old age. The greater rewards tend to go to men rather than to women. Negroes suffer greater social deprivation than whites even when they have the same income. And so on.

From the wide range of possible indicators, five are here chosen to test the relationship of social deprivation to anti-Semitism: race,

(20 per cent). There is not, however, the expected decline with each step up the education ladder. Individuals who did not complete their college education and those who attended business or trade schools are more likely to be anti-Semitic than the group that finished high school. The discrepancy, however, may be more apparent than real. The failure to finish college and the decision to go to business or trade school instead of college are in themselves indicators of relative disprivilege. Comparatively, for example, those who aspire to a high school diploma and acquire it are in this sense privileged relative to those who aspire to a college degree and fail.

sex, age, marital status, and parental background. It was judged that Negroes, women, older people, persons who are widowed, separated, or divorced, and individuals with foreign-born parents are socially deprived relative to their "opposites." The prediction, therefore, is that respondents with these attributes would be the most likely to exhibit anti-Semitism.

TABLE B-4. ANTI-SEMITISM BY LEVEL OF ECONOMIC PRIVILEGE AND OTHER SOCIAL CHARACTERISTICS

Per Cent	*Level of Economic Privilege*[a]			
Anti-Semitic Among:	Low	Medium	High	*Total*
Whites	69%	39%	30%	42%
	(26)	(119)	(111)	(256)
Negroes	56%	42%	[b]	49%
	(34)	(64)	(8)	(106)
Males	59%	39%	27%	39%
	(29)	(83)	(59)	(171)
Females	68%	51%	34%	49%
	(34)	(112)	(58)	(204)
Under 60 years of age	63%	40%	30%	41%
	(51)	(149)	(106)	(306)
Sixty and older	67%	62%	40%	59%
	(12)	(45)	(11)	(68)
Single or married	53%	43%	30%	40%
	(40)	(136)	(106)	(282)
Separated, divorced, widowed	86%	51%	40%	58%
	(21)	(59)	(10)	(90)
Both parents American born[c]	62%	38%	29%	35%
	(13)	(74)	(82)	(169)
One or both parents foreign born	67%	61%	31%	52%
	(15)	(44)	(29)	(88)

[a] Low privilege is defined as a score of zero on the index of economic privilege; medium privilege, as a score of 1 or 2; high privilege, as a score of 3 or 4. Number of respondents in each category shown in parentheses.

[b] Too few cases on which to base a percentage.

[c] Negroes are omitted from this part of the table since in all cases their parents were American born.

As the "Total" column in Table B-4 shows, the expectation is confirmed in every instance. Moreover, with one significant exception, the relation between social deprivation and anti-Semitism is sustained at every level of economic privilege. That is to say, among those who share the same level of economic privilege, respondents who are in a socially deprived category are more anti-Semitic than those who are in a socially privileged category. The only exception is the Negroes. In one of the two possible comparisons, the Negroes are substantially less anti-Semitic than whites; in the other, they are slightly more likely to be anti-Semitic.

The main thrust of Table B-4 is to underscore the strong tendency for anti-Semitism to be associated with both economic and social deprivation. It also shows that economic deprivation is related to anti-Semitism in both the white and Negro communities. However, Negroes are far more socially deprived than whites even when they share the same economic position. From this perspective it is significant that their level of anti-Semitism is, if anything, less than for whites when economic level is controlled. It suggests that the higher rate of anti-Semitism among Negroes revealed in the "Total" column is a result of their extreme economic disadvantage, rather than of some special group quality that leads to heightened hostility toward Jews. In fact, if anything can be attributed to the effect of being Negro per se, it is that it reduces rather than increases the propensity toward anti-Semitism.

Underlying and reinforcing these relationships is the fact that the deprived are less likely to be exposed to what may be described as the enlightened values of the culture. Social and economic deprivation tend to go hand in hand with a kind of cultural deprivation. The data do not allow testing this notion in any comprehensive way but they do give it some confirmation.

One indicator of cultural deprivation, as that concept is being used here, is the number and kind of newspapers a person reads regularly. Those who read no newspapers can be assumed to be culturally deprived relative to regular readers. In Oakland those who read only a local newspaper may be judged to be less culturally privileged than those who read San Francisco papers instead of or in addition to the local press.

As Table B-5 shows, the more economically and socially deprived are indeed less likely to read a newspaper and, when they do, they tend to restrict their reading to the local newspaper. When the relation between newspaper reading and anti-Semitism

TABLE B-5. NEWSPAPER READERSHIP BY LEVEL OF PRIVILEGE

Newspaper Readership	*Level of Privilege*[a] Low	Medium	High	*Total*
Read no newspapers regularly	24%	8%	2%	13%
Read local newspaper only	51	50	38	48
Read San Francisco paper[b]	25	42	60	39
Number	(170)	(173)	(99)	(442)

[a] The general index of privilege is used in this and subsequent tables. This index, it will be recalled from the discussion in chapter 2, also includes sex of respondent as an indicator of privilege.

[b] One or more papers, of which one is a San Francisco paper.

is examined, it is found that the nonreaders are the most likely to be anti-Semitic, and that the readers of a San Francisco paper are the least likely to be so (Table B-6). Respondents who read only a local paper fall between the two extremes.

TABLE B-6. ANTI-SEMITISM BY LEVEL OF PRIVILEGE AND NEWSPAPER READERSHIP

Per Cent Anti-Semitic Among:	*Level of Privilege*[a] Low	Medium	High	*Total*
Non-newspaper readers	70%	46%	[b]	58%
Number	(23)	(13)	(2)	(38)
Readers of local papers only	63%	46%	15%	47%
Number	(70)	(76)	(33)	(179)
Readers of San Francisco paper	42%	40%	33%	38%
Number	(31)	(68)	(54)	(153)

[a] See Table B-5, note a.

[b] Too few cases on which to base a percentage.

The relation is particularly strong among those who scored low on privilege, but holds for the moderately privileged as well. It does not apply, however, to the highly privileged, among whom the relation was reversed. Virtually everyone who scored high on privilege reads a newspaper. For this group, reading a San Francisco newspaper may not be an adequate indicator of cultural privilege.

The only other way that the data allow distinguishing the culturally privileged from the culturally deprived is to use degree of knowledge about the trial itself as an indicator. It will be recalled that the privileged were more likely to be knowledgeable. However, when privilege is controlled, the more the respondent knew about the trial, the less likely he was to be anti-Semitic (Table B-7).

TABLE B-7. ANTI-SEMITISM BY LEVEL OF PRIVILEGE AND KNOWLEDGE OF TRIAL
(per cent anti-Semitic)

		Level of Knowledge		
Level of Privilege	Low	Medium	High	*Total*
Low 0	64% (66)	49% (47)	43% (7)	45% (126)
1	65% (23)	44% (41)	33% (9)	50% (74)
2	41% (17)	40% (25)	28% (25)	36% (67)
3	45% (11)	40% (30)	19% (26)	33% (67)
High 4	50% (8)	35% (17)	22% (23)	31% (48)

This hardly provides sound confirmation of the cultural deprivation hypothesis since it may simply reflect the propensity of the anti-Semitic to avoid exposure to the trial. It is, however, consistent rather than inconsistent with the other evidence and to this extent supports the hypothesis.

It was not a primary or even a secondary purpose of the study of the Eichmann trial to investigate the social sources of anti-Semitism in Oakland. Consequently, the above analysis of the phenomenon is necessarily incomplete. Nevertheless, the effort bore some fruit. It served to validate the measures of anti-Semitism used, and confirmed the role of economic, social, and cultural deprivation in anti-Semitic prejudice.

APPENDIX C

INTERVIEW SCHEDULE

1. The Survey Research Center of the University of California is conducting a public opinion poll throughout Oakland. Here is a list of some recent events that you may have heard about or read about. Would you please tell me whether or not you have heard or read about each one?
   A. The Freedom Riders in the South
   B. The revolution in Uruguay [fictitious]
   C. The American Nazi "Hate Bus"
   D. The death of Gary Cooper
   E. The Tractors-for-Rebels exchange with Cuba
   F. The Bradley kidnaping case [fictitious]
   G. The Eichmann trial
   H. Marilyn Monroe's operation
   I. The death of Ernest Hemingway

   If has heard about Eichmann trial, continue interview.
   If has not *heard about Eichmann trial, skip to question 27.*
2. Do you know whether Eichmann was a Communist, a Nazi, or a Jew?
3. What would you say were the reasons Eichmann was brought to trial? Any other reasons?
4. Do you happen to remember in what country Eichmann was arrested? *If "South America," probe.*
5. And what country arrested him?
6. Do you think it was legal for Israel to bring Eichmann to trial?
7. Is the Eichmann trial over?
   If trial over

Has a verdict been reached?

8. Did the court find Eichmann guilty or not guilty?
   Do you think the court will find Eichmann guilty or not guilty?
   If the court found or will find Eichmann guilty
   And what sentence did the court give him?
   And what sentence do you think the court will give him?
9. Do you yourself think Eichmann is guilty or not guilty?
   If personally thinks Eichmann guilty
   If it were up to you, what sentence would you give Eichmann —death, life imprisonment, imprisonment but not for life, or something else?
10. An *official* estimate has been made of the number of Jews killed by the Nazis before and during World War II. Would you please look at this card and tell me which number comes closest to this official estimate. (*Hand card A.*)
    A. Ten thousand or less (10,000)
    B. One hundred thousand (100,000)
    C. Five hundred thousand (500,000)
    D. One million (1,000,000)
    E. Two million (2,000,000)
    F. Four million (4,000,000)
    G. Six million (6,000,000)
    H. Eight million (8,000,000)
    I. Ten million (10,000,000)
11. As you might have known, the *official* estimate is six million. Do you yourself think this estimate is too high, about right, or too low?
    If thinks too high or too low
    Would you look at the card again and tell me what you think is the real number?
12. (*Hand respondent card B.*) Which of these do you think would have been the right course for the Israeli Government to follow with Eichmann? Please call off the letter opposite your answer.
    A. Try him as they are doing before an Israeli court.
    B. Hand him over to the Germans for trial.
    C. Hand him over to an international court for trial.

D. Let him go free.

13. Do you think it was a good thing that Eichmann was brought to trial or not so good?
(*If good thing or not so good, ask*)
Why do you say that?
14. Suppose other Nazi war criminals accused of persecuting the Jews are caught—do you think they should be let go or do you think they should be brought to trial?
If should be brought to trial
Should they be brought to trial by Israel, by Germany, or by an international court?
15. During the Eichmann trial, Eichmann admitted that he had carried out orders from his superiors to have Jews killed. What would you say about the *way* in which Eichmann carried out these orders—did he do much more than his superiors required, a little more than his superiors required, a little less than his superiors required, or much less than his superiors required?
16. Do you think Eichmann himself killed any Jews?
17. Thinking back to the treatment of the Jews by Nazi Germany *before and during* World War II, do you think the persecution of the Jews was mostly their own fault, partly their own fault, or not at all their own fault?
18. While the Eichmann trial was going on, did you read about it in the newspapers?
If read newspapers or read headlines
About how often did you read about it—every day, once or twice a week, or just once in a while?
19. Did you read about the Eichmann trial in a magazine?
20. Did you hear about the Eichmann trial on the radio?
21. Did you see anything about the Eichmann trial on television?
If saw on television
Did you see any special TV program on the Eichmann trial?
22. Have you talked with anyone about the Eichmann trial?
If has talked with someone about Eichmann trial
Who was that?
Anyone else?

23. How interested would you say you were in the news of this trial—very interested, fairly interested, or not at all interested?
24. Has the Eichmann trial made you feel more sympathetic or less sympathetic toward Israel?
25. Has the Eichmann trial made you feel more sympathetic or less sympathetic toward the Jews?
26. Has the Eichmann trial made you feel more sympathetic or less sympathetic toward the Germans?
27. On each of the cards in this stack is a word or two that are sometimes used to describe different types of people. Please read each of the cards, and then put into one pile the types of people you *yourself* would *like* to have marry into your immediate family, and into the other pile the types of people you would *not like* to have marry into your immediate family. (*Hand cards to respondent to divide into "like" and "not like" piles. If respondent cannot decide on some cards and makes a third pile, let him, but when he is through sorting urge him to separate this third pile into "like" and "not like." If respondent does not know word or words on card, code "don't know." Do not attempt to code during interview. Gather up cards with the "like" and "not like" cards and slip a rubber band around each set for later coding. Code only "don't knows" and "refused" during the interview.*)

RELIGION

Someone who does not believe in God
Someone who never goes to church
Roman Catholic
Jew
Episcopalian
Lutheran
Baptist
Jehovah's Witness
Holy Roller
Buddhist

EDUCATION

Someone who has not finished high school
Someone who has not finished grade school
High school graduate
College graduate

CLASS

Upper class person
Middle class person
Working class person
Lower class person

POLITICAL ORIENTATION
Fascist
Rightwinger
Conservative
Republican
Democrat
Liberal
Leftwinger
Socialist
Communist
Zionist

REGION
Easterner
Southerner
Midwesterner

RACE
Negro
Oriental
White

OCCUPATION
Doctor
Civil engineer
High school teacher
Typist
Watch repairman
Machinist
Assembly-line worker
Longshoreman
Unskilled laborer

NATIONALITY
African
Arab
Japanese
Mexican
Israeli
Polish
Italian
Irish
German
English

28. Here is a card with the names of different groups of people—Negroes, Jews, Catholics, and German-Americans. (*Hand card C.*) Would you please tell me which, if any, of these kinds of people:
    A. Live in your neighborhood?
    B. Have married into your immediate family?
    C. Have been entertained in your home in the past year?
    Are you presently working?
    If working:
    D. Work at the place you work?
    If yes to last question:
    E. Work with you?
29. Now I am going to hand you a sheet with the names of these groups on it and a list of characteristics sometimes used to

describe the groups. Would you please start with the first group and the first characteristic "intelligent" and if you think that "intelligent" describes the majority of Negroes, would you put a check in that box. Then go on to the Jews; if you think that "intelligent" describes the majority of the Jews, you would put a check in that box. If you don't think a characteristic describes a group you would leave the box blank. Go on down and look at each characteristic in turn and check the groups it applies to.

Intelligent
Unclean
Carefree
Honest businessmen
Lazy
Worry too much about what people think of them
Ignorant
Pushy
Clannish
Too aggressive

Now, we are talking to a great many people here in Oakland. We are asking some people for opinions about Catholics, some for opinions about Negroes, some for opinions about Jews, and some for opinions about German-Americans. You happen to fall into the group we want to talk to about the Jews.

30. Some people say that Jews are different from other people. Would you agree or disagree with this statement?
If agree:
In what ways would you say Jews are different from other people?

31. As you may know, many vacation resorts in the United States refuse to accept Jews as guests. Will you please tell me which of these statements comes closest to your own feelings on this matter?
A. Christians have a right to expect that a vacation resort will cater only to other Christians like themselves, or

B. Jews have a right to expect that a vacation resort will accept them on the same basis as Christians.

32. How would you feel if one of the biggest companies in town said it was going to set a limit on the number of Jews it has in the better jobs. Which of these statements comes closest to your feelings on this matter?
    A. I'd think it was a good idea; Jews get more than their share of the better jobs anyway, or
    B. Jews should have the same chance to get the better jobs as anyone else.
33. If a candidate for Congress in this state should declare himself as being against the Jews, would this influence you to vote for him, or against him?
34. Would you vote for a Jew for President of the United States if he were well qualified for this position?

Now, would you please think of your three best friends. *I don't want to know their names,* so let's call them Friend Number 1, Friend Number 2, and Friend Number 3. Let's talk about Friend Number 1 first.

35. Is he a Republican, a Democrat, an independent, or something else?
36. What is his religion? Is he Catholic, Protestant, Jewish, or something else?
    If "Protestant": Do you know what denomination?
37. Do you happen to know what country his family, his ancestors, originally came from?
    If specific country not mentioned:
    Do you know if it was northern Europe, southern Europe, eastern Europe, the Middle East, Africa, or the Orient?
38. Would you say that he and his family are better off financially than you are, about the same, or not as well off?

[*Questions 35–38 were repeated for friends 2 and 3. They were numbered as questions 39–46.*]

Now, I would like to ask you a few questions about yourself.

47. Were you able to get as much schooling as you wanted to?

48. Is this the kind of neighborhood you would like to continue living in?
49. On the whole, are you doing the kind of work you want to do?
50. Would you say that your health is usually excellent, good, fair, or poor?
51. Compared to most people you know, would you say that your family life was very happy, a little happier than average, just about average, or not too happy?
52. How would you say you get along with other people—better, about the same, or worse than most people do?
53. Now I am going to give you another set of cards. These have different sentences on them. Would you please go through this deck of cards and put in one pile the cards you agree with and in the other the cards you disagree with.

    Young people sometimes get rebellious ideas, but as they grow up they ought to get over them and settle down.

    There may be a few exceptions, but in general, Jews are pretty much alike.

    I can't see myself ever marrying outside of my race.

    Most Jews are so Americanized that you can't find anything different about them.

    The trouble with letting Negroes into a nice neighborhood is that they gradually give it a typically Negro atmosphere.

    Every person should have complete faith in some supernatural power whose decisions he obeys without question.

    Sex crimes, such as rape and attacks on children, deserve more than mere imprisonment; such criminals ought to be publicly whipped, or worse.

    What the youth needs most is a strict discipline, rugged determination, and the will to work and fight for family and country.

    Regardless of what some people say, there are certain races in the world that just won't mix with Americans.

The trouble with letting Jews into a nice neighborhood is that they gradually give it a typically Jewish atmosphere.

It would be a mistake ever to have Negroes for foremen and leaders over whites.

Jews don't like to mix with other people so they would rather live in special areas of their own.

There may be a few exceptions, but in general, Negroes are pretty much alike.

Having too many Negroes in a firm is bad for business.

When it comes to the things that count most, all races are certainly not equal.

I can hardly imagine myself marrying a Jew.

If minority groups hope to be liked better, they should first try to get rid of their harmful and irritating faults.

Anyone who employs many people should be careful not to hire a large percentage of Jews.

There is some basic Jewish quality that resists the American melting pot and makes Jews different from other people.

Many of this country's troubles arise from the fact that one minority group controls most of the finance and business.

Anyone who is interested in the best interest of his company wouldn't worry about how many Negroes there were working for him; he would hire on the basis of qualification.

I don't really care if Negroes move into the neighborhood; they're just like anybody else.

People can be divided into two distinct classes: the weak and the strong.

I don't think I could every marry outside of my religion.

One trouble with Jewish businessmen is that they stick together and connive, so that a Gentile doesn't have a fair chance in competition.

Now I would like to ask you a few questions about your background for statistical purposes.

54. Generally speaking, in politics, do you think of yourself as a Republican, a Democrat, an independent, or something else?
55. What was the last grade in school you completed?
56. Are you, or is anyone in your immediate family, a member of a labor union?
57. Do you consider yourself a member of the upper class, the middle class, the working class, or the lower class?
58. Do you own or rent this house (apartment)?
59. What newspapers, if any, do you read regularly? (*Code as many as apply.*) Any others?
60. What magazines do you read regularly?
61. How many years have you lived in Oakland (Piedmont?)
62. Would you tell me the year that you were born?
63. Now, would you tell me where you were born?
64. How large was the community in which you *mainly lived* before you left high school? (*Hand card D.*)
65. And your father, where was he born?
66. And your mother, where was she born?
67. (*Ask all respondents except Negroes.*) From what country did your ancestors *mainly* come?
68. What is your religious preference? (*If Protestant, get denomination.*)
69. In what religion were you raised? (*If Protestant, get denomination.*)
70. How often in the last month did you attend religious services?
71. How important is your religion to you—very important, fairly important, or not too important?
72. Are you presently married?
73. (*If male or single female.*) And what is your occupation?
    (*If married female.*) And what is your husband's occupation?
74. What was your father's occupation when you were in high school (were in your late teens)?

75. (*For all respondents over 21.*) Now would you think for a moment about the family you grew up in. What is the occupation of the brother who was closest to you in age?
(*If no brothers.*) Well, the sister nearest to you in age, what is her husband's occupation?
(*If sister unmarried.*) What is her occupation?
76. Now, I don't want to know your exact income, but would you look at this card (*Hand card E*) and tell me into which of these categories your *family income* falls.

Observation and face sheet data

77. Sex of respondent
78. Race of respondent
79. Neighborhood racial composition
80. Standard of living of respondent
81. Standard of living of neighborhood
82. Type of dwelling
83. Household composition

INDEX

Format by Mort Perry
Set in Linotype Caledonia
Composed, printed and bound by The Haddon Craftsmen, Inc.
HARPER & ROW, PUBLISHERS, INCORPORATED